SYLVIA PLATH

ELISABETH BRONFEN

Northcote House
in association with the
British Council

© Copyright 1998 by Elisabeth Bronfen

First published in 1998 by Northcote House Publishers Ltd, Plymbridge House, Estover Road, Plymouth PL6 7PY, United Kingdom.
Tel: +44 (01752) 202368 Fax: +44 (01752) 202330.

British Library Cataloguing-in-Publication Data
A catalogue record for this book is available from the British Library

ISBN 0 7463 0824 8

Typeset by PDQ Typesetting, Newcastle-under-Lyme
Printed and bound in the United Kingdom

Contents

Acknowledgements

I am very grateful to Isobel Armstrong for having asked me to write this book about Sylvia Plath. The experience has been distressing, compelling, but also enriching. My thanks go to Birgit Erdle, Barbara Straumann, and Benjamin Marius for their encouraging comments on the manuscript. I want to thank Jan Freitag for helping me with the index and Hilary Walford for her work as copy editor.

Finally, my publishers and I gratefully acknowledge the Estate of Sylvia Plath and Faber and Faber Limited for permission to quote from the following works of Sylvia Plath: *The Bell Jar; The Collected Poems* (edited by Ted Hughes); *Johnny Panic and the Bible of Dreams* (introduction by Ted Hughes); *Letters Home: Correspondence 1950–1963;* and *The Journals of Sylvia Plath* (consulting editor Ted Hughes) published by Faber and Faber, London; Random House, New York; and Ted Hughes and Faber and Faber Limited for permission to quote from *The Birthday Letters* (1998).

Biographical Outline

1932   Sylvia Plath is born on 27 October in Boston, the first child of Aurelia Schober and Otto Emil Plath. Her mother is first-generation American, of Austrian descent; her father, Professor of Biology at Boston University, grew up in Poland as the son of German parents and emigrated to the USA at the age of 16.

1937   After the birth of Sylvia's brother, Warren, in 1935, the Plath family moves to the seaside town of Winthrop, Massachusetts, in the close proximity of Sylvia's maternal grandparents.

1940   Otto Emil Plath dies as a result of a leg amputation. For Sylvia this death comes to signify a traumatic disturbance of her childhood existence.

1942   Aurelia Schober Plath moves her family to Wellesley, Massachusetts, and begins working as a High School teacher.

1942–50   Plath attends public schools in Wellesley. She begins to write her first poetry and short stories, occasionally winning contests with these pieces.

1950   Wins a scholarship granted to her by Mrs Olive Higgins Prouty and begins attending Smith College.

1952   With her short story 'Sunday at the Mintons' Plath becomes one of two winners of the *Mademoiselle* fiction competition.

1953   Plath is chosen to go to New York City during the summer to work as one of a select group of American college students as a *Mademoiselle* guest editor. She returns home exhausted and attempts suicide, but is discovered and hospitalized at the psychiatric clinic in Belmont, Massachusetts. She will rework this experience in her novel *The Bell Jar*.

1954   Plath returns to Smith for the second semester. She attends Harvard summer school on a scholarship.

1955   Plath graduates from Smith with a *summa cum laude* degree and prizes for poetry. In October of this year she begins her studies at Newnham College, Cambridge University, on a Fulbright fellowship.

1956   In February Plath meets Ted Hughes, and, after a trip to Germany and Italy with Gordon Lameyer during the spring break, she marries Hughes on 16 June. They spend their honeymoon in Benidorm, Spain. They return to Cambridge and Sylvia finishes her second year as a Fulbright student.

1957   Plath, accompanied by her husband, returns to the USA and begins working as a visiting professor at Smith College.

1958   While living in Boston, where Plath and Hughes decide to dedicate themselves primarily to their writing, she attends Robert Lowell's poetry classes at Boston University, gets seriously involved in therapy, and works as a secretary at the psychiatric clinic of Massachusetts General Hospital.

1959   Ted Hughes and Sylvia Plath travel across the USA and spend two months at the writers' colony Yaddo in Saratoga Springs, NY, before returning to England in December, where they decide to make their home in London.

1960   Plath's first child, Frieda Rebecca, is born on 1 April. In October her first collection of poems, *The Colossus and Other Poems*, is published in England.

1961   At the beginning of the year Plath has a miscarriage, followed by an appendectomy. In August Plath and Hughes move to a house in Devon.

1962   Plath's son, Nicholas Farrar, is born on 17 January. In May *The Colossus and Other Poems* appears in the USA. In October Plath and Hughes separate and in December she moves to London with her children, into the apartment W. B. Yeats had lived in.

1963   Plath's novel *The Bell Jar* is published under the pseudonym Victoria Lucas, in January. On 11 February she commits suicide.

Abbreviations

BJ   *The Bell Jar*, by 'Victoria Lucas' (London: Heinemann, 1963); by Sylvia Plath (London: Faber & Faber, 1966)

CP   *The Collected Poems*, ed. Ted Hughes (New York: Harper & Row, 1981)

JP   *Johnny Panic and the Bible of Dreams: Short Stories, Prose, and Diary Excerpts*, introduction by Ted Hughes (London: Faber & Faber, 1977)

Jour.   *The Journals of Sylvia Plath*, ed. Frances McCullough; consulting ed. Ted Hughes (New York: Random House (Ballantine Press), 1982)

LH   *Letters Home: Correspondence 1950–1963*, selected and edited with a commentary by Aurelia Schober Plath (London: Faber & Faber, 1975)

1

The Plath Myth

Human nature is so well disposed towards those who are in interesting situations, that a young person, who either marries or dies, is sure of being kindly spoken of.

(Jane Austen, *Emma*)

In the spring of 1989 a debate was waged in the *Guardian* over who owns Sylvia Plath's grave. Initially Julia Parnaby and Rachel Wingfield had written a letter to protest that, having travelled to Heptonstall churchyard in Yorkshire so as to visit the grave of the poet, they had found that it was unmarked.[1] They were told the headstone had been removed after repeated vandalization, allegedly by radical feminists objecting to the fact that it commemorates the author as Sylvia Plath Hughes. The absence of this headstone was able to become such an issue of contention, however, because, in addition simply to marking a given burial site, gravestones of celebrities invariably function as a tangible memorial of the deceased for public memory. Marking a grave is meant not only to make sure that the dead poet will not be forgotten but also to designate the manner in which her story is to be remembered. To leave Sylvia Plath's human remains unidentified, claimed Parnaby and Wingfield, could be seen as tantamount to devaluing her work and relegating her to the ranks of the countless culturally productive women who have remained hidden from historical reconstructions of the past. In the course of the following weeks an array of *Guardian* readers either defended the proposed analogy between marking a poet's grave and marking her place in the tradition of women's literature or critiqued this as an untenable assertion. A. Alvarez, along with seven other renowned authors, called upon Ted Hughes and his family to explain the removal of the headstone, implying that this had

1

been done to discourage people from visiting the grave. Ruth Richardson and A. B. Ewen in turn used the debate over Plath's unmarked grave to make a plea for a public memorial to be set up in honour of this poet (be this in Yorkshire or London). Comparing the erection of a funereal memorial with the posthumous publications of her writings, they suggested that the successful management of the corpus of her work by the inheritors of her estate had been conducted at the expense of the former. Other voices, however, rose to criticize, in Margaret Drabble's words, 'this Sylvia Plath graveyard business'; Drabble felt that it was ridiculous to assume a connection between a tangible public sign, marking the dead poet's remains, and the assurance that her work will not vanish from public memory. Equally critical was the plea for silence by William Park, suggesting that any further discussion of Ted Hughes's involvement in the Plath Estate should be stopped once and for all, out of respect both for the living, to whom credit should be given for promoting the work of Plath posthumously, and the dead, who should be left to rest in peace. Finally John Harrison, Vicar of Heptonstall, entered into the arena, offering 'the facts of the matter', by describing the initial burial site, the triple erasure of the lettering 'Hughes' on the headstone, as well as its repeated repair, only to end with a statement of his own indignation: 'it is surely an insult to the dead to use their memorials as a means of political expression.'

The discordant views presented in this debate – a call for a visible tribute to assure the memory of a writer's work, the uncertainty whether a grave is a personal or a public site, as well as whether public memorials of the dead should be appropriated as means of political expression – open further questions. Who or what is being represented by the headstone, given that the deceased in question is not only a public figure but above all the author of seemingly autobiographical texts? Does it recall the historical woman Sylvia Plath? Daughter of Austro-German immigrants, born in Boston in 1932, she had started writing poetry and prose during her adolescence, and won prizes for her creative writing as well as scholarships for her academic excellence, which allowed her to attend first Smith College and then Cambridge University. There she met her future husband, Ted Hughes, with whom she had two children before their marriage broke apart and she ended up committing suicide in 1963. In contrast to her first collection of poems, *The Colossus*, published three years earlier, the poems she had been writing in the months before her suicide exhibited a radical shift in style, which led her former teacher Robert Lowell to comment, 'Everything in these poems is personal, confessional, felt, but the manner of feeling is controlled hallucination, the autobiography of fever.'[2] Or is Sylvia Plath remembered on the headstone as a trope for the woman writer in danger of fading from the literary canon? In other words, does the headstone simply mark the body of the deceased in her absence or does it also function as a screen onto which the fantasies of her survivors can be projected? Does this piece of funerary sculpture, about which so much ado was made, function only as the tangible part of the mourning ritual surrounding Sylvia Plath's death?

Or is it the case that twenty-five years after her suicide her grave had already become what Roland Barthes calls a 'mythic signifier' – a sign, where meaning has left its contingency behind, where history has evaporated, leaving only the letter, which in turn is filled with a second system of values? Describing the rhetorical strategy of the mythic signifier, Barthes argues that, as form puts meaning at a distance, meaning undergoes a rhetorical death,

> but this is a death with reprieve; the meaning loses its value, but keeps its life, from which the form of the myth will draw its nourishment. The meaning will be for the form like an instantaneous reserve of history, a tamed richness, which it is possible to call and dismiss in a sort of rapid alternation: the form must constantly be able to be rooted again in the meaning and to get there what nature it needs for its nutriment; above all, it must be able to hide there.[3]

If, then, the mythic signifier is defined primarily as a constant game of hide-and-seek between meaning and form, with meaning arrested in a state between life and death, neither fully evaporated nor fully visible, Sylvia Plath's grave could be seen as a paradigmatic case for the semiotic transformation at stake. Even while the body of the deceased, and with it the historically contingent 'meaning' of Sylvia Plath's life, has both literally and rhetorically been put at a distance, buried beneath the grave plate, a quarter of a century after her demise it continues to nourish a plethora of narrative 'forms' – biographies, critical studies, readers' responses – whose sustenance require that they feed off this rich material even while keeping it under cover. Indeed, when Ted Hughes finally responded on 20 April 1989, not only did he correct some of the unsubstantiated claims that had been circulated in the course of the 'graveyard business' – notably that Sylvia Plath was not divorced at the time of her suicide. Rather, he also emphasized that what was apparently at stake in the entire affair was the different readers' *mise-en-scène* of desire: 'A rational observer might conclude (correctly in my opinion) that the Fantasia about Sylvia Plath is more needed than the facts. Where that leaves respect for the truth of her life (and of mine), or for her memory, or for the literary tradition, I do not know.'

The problem, of course, is not only that any grave sculpture commemorating a celebrity inevitably enmeshes private with public memory, and in so doing transforms any personal truths of the immediate family into collective narratives that are open to appropriation by friends and strangers alike. Rather, when we are dealing with an author like Sylvia Plath, whose poetic power resides precisely in confessing the most intimate rage publicly and who, in so doing, appeals to our identification with her anguish, our response to her life and her work can never be divorced from fantasy. Furthermore, even if one agrees with Drabble's position that the public commemoration of the resting place of an author's corpse should not be confused with the position this author's corpus takes on in the public's collective memory, the question of whether a grave is marked or not continues, nevertheless, to be significant. It is, after all, a commonplace of anthropology that death, in removing a social being from society, is conceived as a wound both to the family and to the community at large. Not only does the corpse occupy a liminal place, given that the deceased is no longer fully present in the world of the living and about to pass into a state inaccessible to them. Rituals of mourning, falling into two phases, also serve to redress the disempowering cut that the loss of a member entails. By virtue of commemorative representations – of which the headstone is simply the most tangible example – survivors create a new identity for the deceased and reintegrate her back into their community, even while her body disintegrates completely. Indeed, whether they are public or private narratives, the aim of memorial texts thus inevitably consists in preserving an image of the absent person for posterity so as once again to redress the psychic wound death produced. It is crucial, however, that the facts of a life rarely satisfy the desire of the survivors to fill this gap. Rather, the bereaved require narratives that transform the contingency of death into a coherent story, so that memorial texts inevitably say as much about the interests of the tellers who are relating the so-called truth of the life of the deceased than about the deceased herself. As a result, there will always be divergent and perhaps even incompatible descriptions of the life of the deceased competing with each other.

To add to the complexity of posthumous representation one must also bear in mind that the headstone is such a privileged funereal sign precisely because it tangibly performs the fetishistic rhetoric of all commemoration. In Freud's terms, the fetish, as a token of triumph over and safeguard against the threat of castration – for which the sight of absence at the centre of feminine genitalia serves as Western culture's most promi-nent trope – contains a superlative moment of ambivalence, given that the fetish actually sets up a memorial to the threatening body even while it functions as an assuaging substitute of it.[4] As a result, the fetish interlocks the denial of a given body of castrative knowledge with its affirmation. It denies that something is absent from sight by replacing the absent body with a substitute representation. Owing to this substitution, however, the commemorative sign inevitably also points to what is missing. Applying this mode of signification to the rhetoric of the headstone, one could argue that, even while its aim is to assure the reintegration of the deceased into the community of the survivors (thus denying that death calls forth an irrecuperable gap), it always also articulates the irrevocability of this loss. As Jean-Pierre Vernant notes, the headstone holds the place of the deceased as a double, incarnating its life in the beyond. As a sign of an absence, it signifies that death reveals itself precisely as something which is not of this world. In so far as the headstone, in its function of double, marks the site where the dead may be present to the living and the living may project their phantasmatic desires and anxieties onto the dead, it both renders the invisible visible and reveals that the dead belong to an inaccessible realm beyond.[5]

However, given that the headstone functions like a double, meant to replace the body of the deceased (*soma*) by virtue of a grave sign representing her (*sema*), difference is written into its signification from the start. Although it stands in for the deceased, any commemorative text functions as a transformation of the soma into a sign, whose potential meaning is, by definition, plural. Furthermore, the rhetoric of the headstone does not only support the desire of the survivors to transpose historical facts into coherent stories so as to make sense out of the contingency of death. Rather, this translation is particularly poignant given that death has made any direct access to the deceased impossible. Instead, the enigma of the dead body doubled by a headstone poses a hermeneutic task to the survivors. We must read the dead body, and yet, precisely because it is missing, it can neither give answers to our questions nor contradict our speculations. Thus, any readings produced in the wake of death are not only approximations of the truth but also heavily endowed with our fantasies as we transform the particular story of a life into a general narrative befitting our collective-image repertoire. Indeed, as Roland Barthes suggests, 'stereotype is that emplacement of discourse *where the body is missing'*.[6]

While such highly ambivalent rhetoric applies to commemorative representations in general, the case of Sylvia Plath's headstone draws its particular poignancy from the fact that it involves the suicide of a young, gifted author, whose personal and creative potential had not yet been exhausted and who killed herself by placing her head into her stove one night, after having made sure that the gas would not leak out through the door to harm her two small children sleeping in the next room. Not only, then, do legends abound because the premature death of the missing body requires an explanation. Rather, the debate about what name should appear on the headstone, as well as the question whether there should be a shrine or not, can itself be understood as a trope for the way the Plath Estate, the biographers, the critics as well as the readers – all implicated in the act of commemoration – have sought to fill the gap left by this act of suicide. Apparently at stake in the 'Sylvia Plath graveyard business' is not just the question whether she will be forgotten or not, nor which version of the truth of her life is to

6

be preserved for posterity, but rather the troubling recognition that any belated discussion of her is never innocent of the desires of those reading and writing about her. Plath criticism, one could speculate, performs her reader's fantasies, as they project their own desire onto the scenarios staged in her writings as well as the events of her biography. Seeing themselves in this *mise-en-scène*, identifying with it or rather with the persona 'Sylvia Plath' who emerges from this body of writing, readers invest her with the role they would like themselves to play in the fantasy scenario. Her story is so compelling, furthermore, because it points to the inextricable enmeshment between public fortune and private disaster, for the protagonist – the daughter of middle-class European immigrants growing up in Eisenhower's America – was not only socially and professionally highly successful but also appears to have been hopelessly driven towards death.

In their last response to the *Guardian* Parnaby and Wingfield insist that their plea for a suitable commemoration of Sylvia Plath emerges from their feeling that often her 'personal life has overshadowed her genius as a writer' and that their major concern continues to be 'that Sylvia Plath's contribution to literature should have a fitting memorial'. Yet what the repeated vandalization and, in consequence, the repeated removal and reparation of the headstone of Sylvia Plath's grave in part point to is that not only in our reading of her work are we invariably thrown back onto the events of her life, but that in addition any attempt at interpreting her biography along with the body of her work inevitably confronts us with incompatible descriptions of reality. Indeed, what the graveyard debate in the *Guardian* so ingeniously staged is the way her life and her poetry are so inextricably implicated that we can do nothing but read her poetry within the biographical appraisal that has reworked her life for us. As Jacqueline Rose, shrewdly commenting on the entire episode, notes, 'The unintended effect of all this is that it is impossible to read Plath independently of the frame, the surrounding discourses, through which her writing is presented.'[7]

That the debate about the Plath legend should have revolved around an unmarked grave is, however, significant in yet another sense. It is equally a commonplace of anthropology that an unmarked grave points to the fact that the body is not in place, that the boundary between the living and the dead has not fully been drawn, so that a severment of the bond between the deceased and the survivors has not yet been symbolically cemented and the questions her death posed not yet settled. The debate over the marking of Sylvia Plath's grave can, then, also be read as a trope for the manner in which this particular author has taken on an uncanny ghostly existence in our collective-image repertoire. The readers' and critics' fantasy scenario surrounding the life and work of Sylvia Plath involves not only a successful poet driven to suicide at the age of 30 but also an author, speaking from a ghostly position of liminality. Owing to the posthumous publication of a large bulk of her work, though dead she has also been returned to the living, so that she seems to haunt her readers and critics with a spectral voice. In the case of Sylvia Plath, then, death inscribes the body of her writings as a theme – her commemoration of her dead father, her fantasies about her own suicide, her anxieties about the loss of the imagination and of her poetic gift – which she finally came to perform with her own body. Leo Braudy, formulating his own fantasy about the mutual implication between her life and her work, notes: 'Obsessed with the desire for literary fame, Plath wrote about her own death until she succeeded in killing herself. She was the stage manager whose will shaped her work until the play got away from her. The performer can leave the stage – but the person who identifies with the performer often cannot.'[8] Given that a large body of her work became public only when her physical body was already missing, locked away inside a coffin, her celebrity, however, is not only inextricably linked to her suicide. Rather, the question of making present again what is missing owing to death, and, concomitant with this, the issue of stereotyping and fantasy, inevitably inhabit the context within which her texts are read.

What then is the genealogy of the Sylvia Plath myth? The first and most conspicuous voice is, of course, that of Ted Hughes, whose prefaces to a collection of her shorter prose, *Johnny Panic and the Bible of Dreams* (1977), to *The Collected Poems* (1981), and to *The Journals of Sylvia Plath* (1982), as well as whose essays explaining his policy as the editor of her work served as a first insight into the aesthetic and biographic motivations subtending her work. In the narrative he offers as a frame for reading both her poetic and her autobiographical writings Plath emerges as someone imprisoned in a contradictory array of false and provisional selves, which she had to learn to shed before her real self could finally be born in the texts she came to produce in the year preceding her suicide. Accordingly, Ted Hughes considers the majority of her writing to be 'roots only... the biology of Ariel, the ontology of Ariel, the story of Ariel's imprisonment in the pine, before Prospero opened it.'[9] Her poetic root system, he suggests, revolved around the drama of her inner crisis that began with the death of her father, when she was 8, and that found its first acme in her almost successful suicide attempt in the summer of 1953. This psychic 'death', followed by a long period of 'gestation'; or 'regeneration', finally culminated in the psychic 'rebirth' and artistic 'birth of her real poetic voice', which she came to articulate in the poems that were ultimately published under the title *Ariel*. Accordingly, Hughes discusses her poems in relation to the way they fit his narrative about how an old, false self, shattered to the point of being reduced to its essential core, repairs and renovates itself until it is reborn. Concerned with marking the point where her real poetry began, he divides her writing up into root work, interlude pieces, and what he considers to be 'the thing itself'. In so doing, however, he tacitly assumes an alignment between the new self, which had come through a long period of psychic crisis triumphantly, and her new poetic voice, encountering and mastering her psychic terror and hate. The victories achieved in her psychic drama, according to Hughes, served to release her poetic energy, so that finally, 'the *Ariel* voice emerged in full, out of the tree'.[10] This narrative allows him to conclude that 'All her poems are in a sense by-products. Her real creation was that inner gestation and eventual birth of a new self-conquering self, to which her journal bears witness, and which proved itself so overwhelmingly in the *Ariel* poems of 1962.'[11]

By postulating that the importance of her poems lies in registering this psychic development from falsity to authenticity, Ted Hughes, however, himself gave birth to what has continued to vex all subsequent critical readings of Sylvia Plath's work – namely, our inability to sever her psychic life from the body of writing she brought forth. At the same time, admitting that this new self ultimately could not save her, he also inaugurated the troubling question of the relationship between her last poems, so distinctly driven by the energy of hate and her own self-destruction. Yet his narrative inevitably calls forth the question whether the so-called birth of her real poetic self was indeed the result of a psychic rebirth or whether it is possible to apply a more sombre interpretative narrative. This new poetic voice could also be seen as the result of her having fully recognized the horrific truth of her desire for self-expenditure, which in the psychic biography recorded in her *Journals* was clearly as virulent a principle of rendering the contingencies of her life meaningful as her desire for personal acceptance and public renown. Thus, if the *Ariel* poems are read as giving voice to her liberation from all earthly confinement, this radical break with both her past and her world need not only be read as an expression of her movement towards the life of a more authentic self. Rather it could equally be surmised that these last poems derive their unusual force from the recognition that she was already writing on the edge of an open grave; celebrating her own anguish and anger rather than her ability to reconstruct and transform herself.

Sylvia Plath's drive towards death was not only enmeshed with the radical change in poetic voice exhibited in the last poems. Rather in her autobiographical novel *The Bell Jar* her complaint about what it was like to grow up as a middle-class American daughter in the years following the Second World War revolves around her almost successful suicide. It is, then, not surprising that, when A. Alvarez, who had been an ardent supporter of Sylvia Plath's work during her lifetime, wrote *The Savage God*, he should preface this literary study of suicide with a memoir about her death. Presenting his as a counter-narrative to that of Ted Hughes's, he records the transformation of a 'serious, gifted, withheld' young poet, 'still partly under the massive shadow of her husband', into a woman who had outgrown 'the person who had written in that oblique, reticent way' and begun to produce what she considered to be her first genuine body of work.[12] Describing the last time he saw her on Christmas Eve 1962 – 'a priestess emptied out by the rites of her cult' – he insists that her suicide was the result of unfortunate circumstances that prevented her from being saved as she had wanted to be. Accordingly he understands his own rendition to be an antidote to the Plath myth depicting 'the poet as a sacrificial victim, offering herself up for the sake of her art, having been dragged by the Muses to that final altar through every kind of distress'. Precisely because this version misses what he calls 'the courage to turn disaster into art', he proposes his counter-myth – namely, that 'of an enormously gifted poet whose death came carelessly, by mistake, and too soon'.[13] However, against his conscious intentions, Plath's death drive, which is to be disavowed, is also obliquely acknowledged. Even if Alvarez maintains that 'the suicide adds nothing at all to the poetry', his insistence that Plath be seen not as the passive victim of her self-destructive tendencies but rather as the victim of tragic circumstances denies her any agency in her act of suicide. More importantly, it serves once again to weld her work to the failure of her gamble with death.

As Janet Malcolm notes, 'How the child, plump and golden in America, became the woman, thin and white in Europe, who wrote poems like 'Lady Lazarus' and 'Daddy' and 'Edge', remains an enigma of literary history, one that is at the heart of the nervous urgency that drives the Plath biographical enterprise, and of the hold that the Plath legend continues to exert on our imaginations.'[14] Critics have taken on different positions in response to this myth, which has Sylvia Plath, having returned to the continent of her ancestors, on the one hand liberating herself Ariel-like from her courtship with death, her authentic self and poetic voice finally born, and, on the other, embodying a phoenix-like transformation, where the docile housewife has turned into a powerful angry poet, abandoned by her husband and writing her great work on the brink of physical and psychic disaster. In both cases, as Jacqueline Rose points out, the Plath myth 'presents all Plath's work in terms of a constant teleological reference to *Ariel*', with all other aspects of her writing by-products, at the same time that its other teleological reference point is the strange last days of her life when, hovering between life and death, she so feverishly wrote her most poignant poetry.[15] Feminist critic Ellen Moers, concerned with the question of how to rewrite the canon of English literature so as to include literary women, simply proclaimed, 'No writer has meant more to the current feminist movement, though Plath was hardly a "movement" person, and she died at age thirty before it began.[16] While Moers simply points to Sylvia Plath's case as an illustration of the difficulties facing the woman writer, without offering any detailed discussion of her work, Sandra M. Gilbert merges her feminist concern with Ted Hughes's narrative of artistic death and rebirth.

> The Plath myth [she argues] began with an initiation rite described in the pages of *Seventeen*, and continued with the introduction into the fashionable world of *Mademoiselle* that is examined in *The Bell Jar*, and with the publication of doggedly symmetrical poems, and the marriage in a foreign country, and the births of two babies, to the final flight of *Ariel* and the dénouement in the oven and all the rest.[17]

What makes this myth so compelling, according to Gilbert, is that the manner in which Plath transcribes her autobiographical concerns into poetry and prose actually follows the pattern of nineteenth-century women's fiction, such as *Jane Eyre*. Modelled along the trajectory of Charlotte Brontë's protagonist, 'being enclosed...and then being liberated from an enclosure by a maddened or suicidal or "hairy and ugly" avatar of the self is', according to Gilbert, 'at the heart of the myth that we piece together from Plath's poetry.'[18] Yet, in contrast to the stories of her nineteenth-century literary predecessor, what Plath's biography comes above all to stand for is the impasse of female creativity that runs counter to the achievements of feminism in the twentieth century. Torn between a longing for the freedom of flight and a fear of the risks of this freedom in a different way from that of either Jane Eyre or her literary sister Catherine Earnshaw Heathcliffe, Sylvia Plath embodies a paradigmatic case for feminism because 'her desire for stasis, her sense of her ancestry, her devotion to the house in which she has lived' and the urgency to construct a self outside this cultural and psychic confinement exemplify how, in real life, there was often no way out for women writers. Gilbert thus inadvertently returns to the myth of the poet sacrificing herself for her art when she concludes – 'out of the plaster of the past, these poems fly, pure and new as babies. Fly, redeemed – even if their mother was not – into the cauldron of morning.' Linking the dead body of the poet with the body of writing, she presents Sylvia Plath as standing in for two crucial aspects of our Western cultural myths about the woman writer: the social and psychic constraints imposed upon feminine authorship and the tragic aporia that, while the corpus survives, it often does so at the cost of the author's life.

In sharp contrast, though also writing out of a feminist concern, Linda Wagner pits her introduction to her anthology, *Critical Essays on Sylvia Plath*, against the Plath legend that has constructed her as a 'possessed poet', and instead claims that we should pay critical attention exclusively to her talent, to her poetic skill, to her appreciation by other poets, and, finally, to her diligent single-mindedness as an author.[19] According to Wagner, cultivating a blindness towards the suicidal aspect of Plath's work offers us the valuable insight into her as a survivor, so that the Sylvia Plath emerging from this depathologizing, though not demythologizing narrative, is a woman using her writing to face, explore, and work through the conflict between the various identities she had to choose from – professionalism, authorship, domesticity, maternity. However, while Wagner in her counter-narrative reads Sylvia Plath as the survivor of an unresolvable cultural dilemma, other critics have, in turn, focused on the discrepancies inscribed in the persona that emerges from the poetry. In these critical narratives, Sylvia Plath is seen as staging rather than resolving the psychic and cultural dilemma of the writing daughter. As Harold Fromm surmises, 'she entertained virtually every possible self, from virginal pious daughter to roaring bitch to moon-goddess to adoring mother, and...none of these selves can be accorded more authentic priority than any of the others'.[20] One could, then, speculate whether our fascination for the Plath myth might not arise from the way in which, confronted with the choice of admiring her poetry stripped entirely of its biographical context and reading her poetic craft within the frame of psychic disturbance and multiply self-fashionings, we are forced to recognize that hers may well be an undecidable case. Indeed Anne Stevenson, defending herself against the vitriolic criticism her biography *Bitter Fame* received, astutely asks,

> Why does her appeal so much affect us? What spell does this tragic victim – of what, of whom? – still exert over us? Why does a poet...whose death was hardly noticed except by her devastated family and friends – why does this tragically dead young woman

13

still rise in her powerful writings, pathetically, aggressively, to make converts for or against her in a never-concluded war between her side and the Other's?[21]

The answer Stevenson offers in defence of her biography, however, significantly lies in the move towards the mythic, for, even though she begins by discussing the cultural milieu that influenced Plath's work, as well as the cultural movements such as feminism her writing in turn came to influence, she ends up by locating the power of this author's appeal in 'the universality of those black, despondent, irrational states of mind she so convincingly reveals in her uniquely strong, vivid language'.[22] Once again, historically contingent meaning is dissipated, substituting the missing body with a trope, which in turn is filled with a second, essentializing, system of meaning.

Even when one looks at critics less concerned with perpetrating, critiquing, or rewriting the Plath myth, the spirit of undecidability reigns. George Steiner, faulting her for her 'angular mannerisms, her elisions and monotonies of deepening rhyme', also praises her for 'the need of a superbly intelligent, highly literate young woman to cry out about her especial being, about the tyrannies of blood and gland, of nervous spasm and sweating skin, the rankness of sex and childbirth in which a woman is still compelled to be wholly of her organic condition'.[23] However, even though he focuses on the specific bodiliness of her poetic themes, he does so only to end up by locating a universalizing feminine condition in such a concentration on the body. Equally restrained in her estimation of the poetic merits of Sylvia Plath, Marjorie G. Perloff, finding her imaginative world 'essentially a limited one', nevertheless turns back to the biographical authenticity informing these texts so as to conclude that she 'will be remembered less for a major œuvre than for a handful of astonishing and brilliant poems, a fascinating autobiographical novel, and for the example of her life with its terrible tension between success and suffering – a tension peculiarly representative of her time and her place'.[24] Irwing Howe, explicitly giving his critical reading the subtitle 'A Partial Dissent', suggests that there is 'something monstrous, utterly disproportionate' in her appropriation of holocaust imagery for a discussion of her relationship to her father. Yet significantly he ends his piece by praising Plath for the poems, which, according to him, she produced when, having abandoned the confessional mode, she wrote out of a 'strange equilibrium', 'a hallucinatory, self-contained fervour', a 'voice unmodulated and asocial', positioned 'in some mediate province between living and dying...balancing coolly the claims of the two', giving voice to 'a different kind of existence, at ease at the gate of dying'.[25] What is compelling for Howe is precisely not a historic contextualization of death by an American of German–Austrian origins, writing in her self-chosen British exile, nor the concretely biographical proclamation of the daughter's discontent, resentment, and anger, but rather the quiet resignation of the disembodied poet's voice, speaking at the boundary of nonexistence, so that once again any historically contingent meaning has been arrested in a state between life and death.

There are, of course, other critical voices, seeking to deplete the Plath myth itself of its nourishment. In this vein Elizabeth Hardwick suggests that, by choosing to write about death, rage, hatred, psychic and bodily wounds, deformities, suicide attempts, fevers, and operations, Plath 'has the rarity of being, in her work at least, never a "nice person"'. Far from ascribing to her a 'mystical and schizophrenic vagueness', a 'dreamy loss of connection', as those do who turn her into an authentic priestess of worldlessness, Hardwick instead sees her as 'all strength, ego, drive, endurance', 'capable of anything' in her destructiveness towards herself and others, merciless in her self-absorption, and in her death 'alone, exhausted from writing, miserable – but triumphant too, achieved, defined and defiant'.[26] Although she also acknowledges that 'the suicide of a young woman with the highest gifts is inevitably a circumstance of the most moving and dramatic sort', so that 'we cannot truly separate the work from the fascination and horror of the death', Hardwick, nevertheless, counters this pull towards biographic fatality by advocating we read Sylvia Plath's poems about her fascination with death and pain, about her vulnerability, her rage, and her combative spirit, 'as if she were still alive'.[27] Equally annoyed at the way Sylvia Plath's work is always read in tandem with the individual critic's responses to her suicide, Katha Pollitt voices her hope that the publication of *The Collected Poems* should redress such a reductive approach, by illustrating not only her craftsmanship but also her consistent movement towards 'greater daring and individuality'.[28] Following Hard-wick's suggestions that we screen out the suicide as the reference against which all her work is measured, Pollitt concludes with her own recuperative fantasy – namely, that, had Sylvia Plath not died, her drive towards transgressing poetic limits would have lead to further self-transformations.

Yet apparently, in the case of Sylvia Plath, the biographic urge is insurmountable. Commenting on the way Plath devotees inevitably read her work as the result of a tension between poetic power or pathology, as a harbinger of her suicide, as an articulation of the confinement imposed upon her by her sex and her liberation from this constraint, Bruce Bawer dispara-gingly suggests that, 'patently, the real interest lies not in Plath's art but in her life', which, he adds, 'is fascinating as a study in the nexus among art, ambition and abnormal psychology, and, more specifically, in the formation of an author whose most anguished poems, composed only weeks before her suicide, are widely considered to be the quintessence of confessional poetry'.[29] While the poems preceding *Ariel* seem to him to be 'more skilful than inspired', often reading 'like descriptive exercises', exhibiting a 'laboured quality, a manufactured intensity, their savage images striking one as over-wrought and self-conscious, their ire and loathing coming across as false', he admits that the late poems are 'often quite effective, by way of natural language and rhythms, manically insistent repetitions and multiple rhymes, and sensational, often surrealist images'. Nevertheless, because he ultimately judges them to be 'less a breakthrough than a breakdown', he, too, ultimately privileges the life over the aesthetic significance of the work: 'The biographies of Plath', he concludes, 'make it clear that these poems are the work of a psychologically complicated and fascinating woman; but the poems themselves are, by compar-ison to the woman, woefully simple and – after the first reading – progressively less interesting.'[30] Far less harsh in her aesthetic judgement, yet responding to the way in which the Plath myth has served such a plethora of identifactory projections, Janet Malcolm also soberly concludes, 'it has frequently been asked whether the poetry of Plath would have so aroused the attention of the world if Plath had not killed herself. I would agree with those who say no. The death-ridden poems move us and

electrify us because of our knowledge of what happened...
When Plath is talking about the death wish, she knows what she
is talking about.'[31]

What these discordant critical voices – speaking for Sylvia Plath,
who, because her suicide preceded her celebrity, could never
speak for herself – ultimately illustrate is that we cannot decide
once and for all what is ultimately a question of aesthetic taste –
namely, whether she is indeed one of the major voices in post-
war British-American poetry, or whether she is merely a minor
poet with an unusual biography. Rather, regardless of her
aesthetic value and regardless of how we read the relationship
between her suicide and the powerful poetic force with which
she came to proclaim her anguish and her anger, Sylvia Plath
does matter to us precisely because her life and her work
mutually authenticate each other in such a troubled, yet also
resilient manner. Indeed we care enough about the Plath myth
that our hunger for ever new biographies seems to be insatiable.
Given that they arrest historically contingent meaning in a state
between life and death, with the concrete history neither fully
evaporated nor fully visible, one could say these biographies
strangely conform to the rhetoric of what Barthes calls myths of
everyday culture. Not only do they offer a death with reprieve,
because they resurrect an image of the dead author from beyond
the grave. Each biography also feeds off historical material, only
to turn it into a narrative where meaning has left its contingency
behind, having translated it into a coherent narrative, which
offers a particular biographer's version of this author's life.
However, even while in the course of narrative transformation
contingent meaning loses its value, it is nevertheless also kept
alive as the nourishing matrix upon which each new biography
can be grounded.

Looking at the publication history of Sylvia Plath's work, it is
indeed striking, how, from the start, the posthumous edition of
her texts went hand in hand with intermittent revelations of bits
and pieces of biographical material, so that the full meaning of
her life neither became entirely visible nor was it ever totally
dissipated. During her lifetime Sylvia Plath had her stories as
well as her poetry accepted by a wide range of British and
American journals, include the *New Yorker*, *London Magazine*, the

London Observer, Mademoiselle, and *Ladies Home Journal,* and had published both a first collection of poems under the title *The Colossus and Other Poems* (in 1960 with Heinemann in London and in 1962 with Knopf in New York), as well as her novel *The Bell Jar* under the pseudonym Victoria Lucas (a month before her death in 1963, with her British publisher). *Ariel,* the first of the posthumous texts, was published both in England and in the United States in 1966, in a version put together by Ted Hughes, which diverged somewhat in content and arrangement from the volume she had initially intended to publish, excluding poems Hughes had found to be inappropriately aggressive. While *The Bell Jar* was republished in England one year later, now under her real name, her mother Aurelia Schober Plath successfully delayed its American publication for six years. Harper & Row published it in 1971, along with an appendix containing eight original Plath pen-and-ink drawings and a biographical afterword by Lois Ames, revealing for the first time some of the details of Sylvia Plath's private life, so as to convince the American public that the novel be read first and foremost as an autobiographic narrative. In response to the American publication of her daughter's unabashedly critical representation of the maternal figure, Aurelia Schober Plath decided to publish a selection of the letters her daughter had written to her between 1950 and 1963 under the title *Letters Home.* In 1966 Charles Newman had already dedicated an issue of *TriQuarterly* to a commemoration of Sylvia Plath, asking those who had known her, notably Ted Hughes, Anne Sexton, Lois Ames, and A. E. Dyson, to offer an evaluation of her work along with their personal reminiscences.[32] Meanwhile Ted Hughes had decided to publish two further collections of poems in 1971 – *Crossing the Water* and *Winter Trees* – which contained poems written between the *Colossus* and the *Ariel* poems, as well as those poems which had been left out of his edition of *Ariel.* Finally Hughes published *The Collected Poems* in 1981, for which Sylvia Plath was posthumously awarded the Pulizter Prize and, in part as a response to Aurelia Schober Plath's edition of the *Letters Home,* he served as consulting editor to an edition of *The Journals of Sylvia Plath* by Frances McCullough, published only in the United States in 1982. In the decade following A. Alvarez's memoir of Sylvia Plath in *The Savage God,* several further memoirs and biographies appeared: Nancy Hunter Steiner's *A Closer Look at Ariel* (1973), describing her friendship with Plath at Smith College and during one summer at Harvard, as well as Eileen Aird's first biographical and critical study *Sylvia Plath* (1973). Since the mid-1970s, five biographies have appeared – Edward Butscher's *Sylvia Plath: Method and Madness* (1976), emphasizing the multiple roles she came to assume, the girl, the poet, and the bitch-goddess; Linda Wagner-Martin's *Sylvia Plath: A Biography* (1987), concentrating on the conflicts facing her as a woman writer; Anne Stevenson's *Bitter Fame: A Life of Sylvia Plath* (1989), highlighting all her ruthlessly self-absorbed traits, her ambitions, her jealousies, and her psychic fragility; Ronald Hayman's *The Death and Life of Sylvia Plath* (1991), presenting her as the damaged, passive victim of the men in her life, from her father to her husband; and Paul Alexander's *Rough Magic: A Biography of Sylvia Plath* (1991), focusing on her fascination for violence at the heart of all her relationships and her art.

That the question who owns the facts of Sylvia Plath's life – her family or the public – has no simple answer became evident when, six months after the heated exchange over her unmarked grave, a new debate broke out in response to Anne Stevenson's *Bitter Fame*, the biography officially sanctioned by the Plath Estate. In the author's note introducing her preface, Stevenson had openly admitted, 'In writing this biography, I have received a great deal of help from Olwyn Hughes, literary agent to the Estate of Sylvia Plath. Ms. Hughes's contributions to the text have made it almost a work of dual authorship.'[33] Many reviewers consequently took Stevenson to task not so much for her interest in deidolizing Sylvia Plath by foregrounding her unattractive sides as well as her psychic instability – allegedly evidenced by vengeful jealousy, success-hunger, manipulative self-obsession and suicidal tendencies – but more importantly for giving in to the interference by the Plath Estate. Including, as an appendix, personal testimonies by Lucas Myers, Dido Merwin, and Richard Murphy, all of whom felt little sympathy for Sylvia Plath during her lifetime, the biography Anne Stevenson ended up writing turned into a flawed hybrid – ambivalently wavering between the biographers' opinion and the Estate's preferred interpretation of the events. If the other biographies had perhaps privileged the opinions of those family members and friends who were interested in offering a favourable representation of the deceased, Stevenson staunchly omitted any voices that would have taken Plath's side on such controversial issues as her marriage, her career, and her psychic distress. The accusations of interference that consequently surfaced in the press led Ted Hughes to respond with a letter to the *Observer*, published on 29 October 1989, in which he vehemently denied the charges made against him and the Estate of suppressing vital materials about Sylvia Plath. Instead, he repeatedly insisted that his actions were dictated by an awareness that one must take 'responsibility for the real consequences of words', so as not only to protect the surviving family and friends from having yet more 'pain and bitterness' injected into their lives but also to protect the Estate from libel suits. Yet what understandably appears as a strategy of self-protection to those directly involved can equally appear to the critical onlooker like a manipulative strategy, meant to assure the Estate of the self-representation it seeks to maintain. Perhaps precisely because material has not been revealed (though partially open to scholars in the Rare Book Room of Smith College), in any case held back so that its public circulation might be prohibited, the Plath myth has had such appeal. Analogous to the absent Sylvia Plath, who can no longer respond to the charges of the testimonials made about her, the absent body of writing evokes ever more conjectures and allegations. Because we are led to believe that we have not yet been given all, so that concomitantly we can cherish the fantasy that the lost journals and the lost novel might still resurface, we do not seem to tire mulling over ever new details of this strangely enmeshed body of creative and autobiographical texts. Even if the editors remove certain passages distasteful to them (be this Plath's mother in the case of the *Letters Home*, or Plath's husband in the case of *The Journals*), the ellipses, marked as [omission], explicitly point to the fact that something has been excluded, and, because something is marked as missing, we imagine what might be there. Haunted by this gap in knowledge, we fantasize that the key to the secret of Sylvia Plath might still be found, that the facts that will make everything clear may still be uncovered, that historically contingent meaning might finally fully come to rest in the completely coherent last narrative solution.

Thus the Plath scholar Mary Lynn Broe used her review of the recent surge in Plath biographies once more to take issue with the Plath Estate for its 'disturbing editorial and censorship practices' which she locates in the 'sheer volume of excisions, omissions, variant editions, and explanatory notes' that have accompanied the rearrangement of the *Ariel* poems and the two other collections, the cuttings from the published *Journals*, in the 'disappearance, destruction, or simply nonpublication of many of Plath's own writings from 1962–1963', and its intervention in all critical reappraisal of her life and her work.[34] Jacqueline Rose's *The Haunting of Sylvia Plath* appeared as the long-awaited critical response to the impasse of Sylvia Plath criticism – bent on discovering the truth about her last day, when, at the height of one of the coldest winters in London, separated from her husband, she feverishly wrote those astonishing final poems. Critics have found themselves caught up in offering either hostile representations of Sylvia Plath as a literary *femme fatale*, the destroyer of men, and the victim of her own destructive passions, so as to vindicate her husband and the interventions of the Plath Estate, or a sympathetic representation of her as having been destroyed by her family as well as the circumstances of her life, but doing so at the cost of blaming Ted Hughes for everything from psychic and physical abuse to a misuse of his function as literary executor. Recognizing that it is often 'technically impossible to separate Plath's voice from those who speak for her'[35] yet seeking to move beyond any ideological alliance – be this the camp that pathologizes Plath or the one that idolizes her as the victim of a patriarchal world – Rose works against the desire of most critics to produce a unified and consistent version of Sylvia Plath as an author and a woman, focusing instead on the unsettling and irreducible dimensions of psychic processes she came to articulate in the body of her writing. Given, then, that we know Plath only through her own writing and what has been written about her, Rose's challenging wager is that 'Plath is a fantasy, she writes fantasy. She is a symptom, she writes the symptom... she haunts and is haunted by the culture; she writes of those most traumatic historical moments when a culture comes to haunt – can only become a phantom of – itself.'[36]

In her chapter 'The Archive', responding to Ted Hughes's claim in a letter to the *Independent* (20 April 1989) 'I hope each of us owns the facts of her or his own life', Rose argues that, in the case of Sylvia Plath, such ownership is 'a war in which husbands and wives, mothers and daughters battle over the possession of – or rather, the constitution of what will pass *as* – the truth'.[37] She continues that what is perhaps so troubling about the publishing policy of the Plath Estate is not, as Broe maintains, that material has been omitted or presented within the context of editorial commentary meant to control the interpretation of these texts. Problematic instead is the fact that her autobiographical writings along with a large bulk of her poems, none of them intended for publication, were ever published at all. This leads to the troubled yet also compelling situation that Sylvia Plath emerges from her own writing as a highly ambivalent and inconsistent figure, where it is impossible to say with certainty which version of a story is true, which version of her self is authentic, but in all cases defying the desire for a coherent final narrative, which would be possible only by virtue of omissions. Ironically a complete picture is never a coherent one. As Rose concludes, 'to try to construct a single, consistent image of Plath becomes meaningless, not just because of the vested interests that so often appear to be at stake in the various attempts to do so that we have seen, but far more because the multiplicity of representations that Plath offers of herself make such an effort so futile.'[38]

Coming late to the game played for the truth of Sylvia Plath's life, and recognizing that, like all the other players, she can be neither innocent nor impartial, Janet Malcolm turned the screw of interpretation yet another degree by insisting on 'the psychological impossibility of a writer's not taking sides'.[39] Thus, seeking to counter what she perceives as 'the public's need to see Plath as victim' – and so choosing to side with the dead over the living because, as survivors, we invariably identify with their helplessness, passivity, and vulnerability – Malcolm openly admits her partiality to Ted and Olwyn Hughes. Yet ultimately at stake for her in the Sylvia Plath game is the way our cultural obsession with this myth does not only reside in the jarring disparity between the life and the work, nor in the fact that the biographers, seeking to find a key to her suicide, to the source of her art, and to the ambiguity of her person, end up with incongruent interpretations. Rather, the unresolved kernel of apparently hidden knowledge that keeps eliciting ever new interpretations, she suggests, is a fallibility built into the very project of biography itself: 'The many voices in which the dead girl spoke – the voices of the journals, of her letters, of *The Bell Jar*, of the short stories, of the early poems, of the *Ariel* poems – mocked the whole idea of biographical narrative.'[40] There can be no single and unequivocally truthful representation of a deceased poet, because the object of the biographical study – the woman Sylvia Plath as she came to fashion herself in a myriad of texts – offers such highly disparate representations of herself. Malcolm, therefore, not only asks us to reflect upon our own implication in any interpretation we choose to privilege, but, perhaps more importantly, beckons us to explore Sylvia Plath's multivocal texts precisely not for the way they might allow the critic to construct a coherent integrated self but rather for the way they so alluringly but also so disturbingly offer a full record of Sylvia Plath's irresolvable ambivalence.

In January 1998 Ted Hughes astonished the literary community by publishing eighty-eight poems about his relationship with Sylvia Plath, which he had written at intervals and without confiding in anyone over the previous twenty-five years. Conceived as an apostrophe to the deceased, whom he evokes so that her presence might serve as a source for his poetic inspiration, *Birthday Letters* is written in the second-person present. Hughes speaks to Sylvia Plath as though she were still alive, as though they were looking back on their shared past together. Manipulating the structure of direct address in a fictionalized way so as to allow for the impossible – the resurrection in fantasy of someone dead – he promises to give account of a particularly painful and haunting chapter of his life. However, if in the course of this rhetorical gesture, as Barbara Johnson notes, 'the absent, dead, or inanimate entity addressed is thereby made present, animate, and anthropomorphic', one must not forget that apostrophe 'is a form of ventriloquism through which the speaker throws voice, life, and human form into the addressee, turning its silence into mute responsiveness.'[41] Indeed, the reanimation inherent in this rhetorical mode allows Hughes to appropriate Plath's silence – a 'stillness that neither | Of us can disturb or escape' – so as to legitimize his version of their shared life. It is as if, having her present again, he can use this digression from straight speech finally to tell his version of what happened. In her function as muse – thus the strange logic of the apostrophe – Sylvia Plath calls forth vignettes from their daily life which allow him to give voice to his anguish and sorrow over her death, but also to his sense of having been betrayed, because he was struck by her violent fury, and drawn with her into death's force field. Repeatedly he casts himself as the one she had to hit first, before she could reach her real goal, her 'Daddy', the 'god with the smoking gun'.[42] Implicitly, then, he uses the reanimation of his first wife to voice his complaint that, in her psychic reality, he was never anything other than a paternal surrogate. In the one poem where he invokes his rival, Otto, he notes how the ghost of his wife's dead father was inseparable from his own shadow, and accuses him, 'I was a whole myth too late to replace you'[43] – as though to relieve himself of the guilt of having failed to ward off her death.

Birthday Letters asks, therefore, to be read not only as a commemoration of Sylvia Plath but perhaps more crucially as the work of Ted Hughes's mourning. By transforming the contingency of death into a coherent narrative about their passionate meeting, their tempestuous marriage, as well as his inability to ease her obsession with her father and with writing until these two enmeshed death forces ultimately came to consume her, he can finally set the furies that have haunted him since her demise at rest. Beginning with the very first poem, in which he describes how he first spotted her in a photograph of the Fulbright scholars that were coming to Cambridge that year, the narrative he has to tell is marked by a fatal destiny. Even during their phase of courtship, the body he desires, though standing before him as a 'rubbery ball of joy', 'slim and lithe and smooth as a fish', representing a new, American world he can only marvel at, is irrevocably marked by scars that recall her past madness and suicidal urges. During their very first embrace he recalls hearing a sober star, whispering to him 'stay clear'.[44] The image of Sylvia Plath that emerges in these *Birthday Letters* is, then, of one who is being eaten alive by the dangerous fiction she has created in relation to her mother and father, while he is nothing but a protective shield between the woman he loves and the dead father to whom she is so fatally drawn. Throughout the narrative we thus find scenes illustrating her exuberant, indeed reckless appetite for life balanced by others focusing on her exaggerated dependence on and her irrational jealousy of him. Then again we are presented scenes in which he nurses her during a fever or is able to keep the demons that haunt her at bay, especially in the poems recalling her pleasure at childbirth and happy moments shared with her children. All these scenes, however, are recollected under the sign of an omen, regardless of whether this takes the shape of her unsatiable ambition, the panic and fear that came in tandem with her writing, or ultimately her obsession with death itself.

As the narrative progresses, Ted Hughes emerges more and more as the impotent rival who, far from being able to help her escape from her fascination with death, actually serves as the unwitting body over whom the paternal figure of death comes to be resurrected; either because as a surrogate love object he recalls the father she had lost or because, in calling upon her to write, he in fact encourages her imaginative encounter with this lethal predecessor. Describing how he built her a writing table leads him to recognize that in so doing he gave her an entrance into precisely the underworld from which 'Daddy' came so uncannily to be resurrected. In so doing, however, Hughes addresses the devastating aporia at the heart of these birthday missives. Unable to hold out against the power of his spectral rival, he finds himself in the role of the helpless onlooker, who, though unable to ward off catastrophe is, nevertheless, also implicated: 'Finding your father for you and then | Leaving you to him.'[45] Even though he can glimpse the ogre that hides in the forty-ninth room of her palace, which she had for a long time successfully kept locked, he can never fully understand its power. Yet, bound to her in marriage, he, too, is sentenced by this fate, in part, because he is arrested in a state of sharing a secret he does not fully grasp. Recalling her first day of teaching at Smith College and the helpless terror she felt, the two time frames merge as the girl, of whom he knows she is going to die, transforms into the corpse he cannot forget:

> But then I sat, stilled,
> Unable to fathom what stilled you
> As I looked at you, as I am stilled
> Permanently now, permanently
> Bending so briefly at your open coffin.[46]

25

But he is also irrevocably struck by the fatedness of his wife because, even while he can use his narrative of their shared life to fashion a story that will relieve him of his oblique guilt, he can do so only by recognizing that, in her agony, which was also the source of her poetic power, he never played anything other than a supporting part. The flames that finally consume her are brought about by her urge to shape into a story the traumatic knowledge of the past she could and would not shed. It is only fitting that, in the final poem of the collection, Ted Hughes addresses his wife's sense of colour only to voice, in a note merging accusation with resignation, that by exchanging a 'bone-clinic whiteness' for a 'pit of red' – the latter signifying a wound that will not close – the jewel she lost was her sense of the colour blue, reminiscent of the ocean, the site of safety but also the site which in her personal mythology had come to harbour her father. In so far as his poetic defence offers any apology to those who hold him at least in part responsible for her death, it takes the form of declaring his own fallibility in the face of her obsession with her dead father and with death itself.

And yet, if apostrophe allows the poet to ventriloquize the absent addressee, his own poetic voice seems to be infected by the exchange as well. While the dead beloved, functioning as muse for the poetic utterances of a mourning lover, is a literary topos well known to us – from Dante's invocation of Beatrice, to Poe's obsession with Virginia Clemm, and Henry James's recasting of his necrophilic desire for Minny Temple in novels such as *Wings of the Dove* – the unusual turn Ted Hughes gives this poetic convention is that he explicitly refers to the texts written by the dead woman. He casts himself as one who has been both consumed by her death and the furies that have haunted him since, and also infected by her texts. In one of the first poems he describes how reading her journal entry allows him to recall the nocturnal scene where he missed meeting her. Indeed, in the course of his poetic narrative he articulates how her reformulation of shared experiences in her journal entries or poems not only diverged from his perception at the time but in hindsight also allowed him to recognize what at the time he had missed or misunderstood, notably her psychic anguish, torture, and the inherited traumatic knowledge that cryptonymically came to haunt her. While he openly admits that he came to see the world anew through her eyes, he also insists that – in part owing to their cultural difference, in part owing to her parental debt – he often could not share her fated vision of places and events. Yet part of his appropriation of the deceased not only involves commenting on her journal entries but also imitating her poetic voice. In doing so, he does not only undo temporality, speaking as she did in the past. Rather, he uses ventriloquism to offer his version of poems, such as 'Daddy', 'Ariel', or 'Rabbit-Catcher', the bone of so much critical contention. One could surmise that, much as he sought to control the Plath Estate, and with it the memory and reputation of his dead wife, with these poetic refigurations of scenes from the poems and journals he also seeks to control the correct interpretation of her texts. But – and herein lies the paradox of the elegiac apostrophic mode – the voice of the survivor is never more than a supplement. Even if it seeks to supersede the deceased, it feeds off this host, and lives only in relation to the texts that have gone before it.

The sober honesty irrevocably written into this project of reanimation and recollection ultimately resides in the terrible fact that he, who has clearly been marked by this death, cannot give us the answer to it. His collection of poems is a gift to us, not because it solves the mystery about Sylvia Plath's enmeshment of a death drive with poetic power, but precisely because it preserves the fascination, which this myth exerts on our fantasy, as an irresolvable clandestine knowledge, as a secret we share. A talented woman who dies at 30 remains in the memory of those who survive her preserved in an open grave. Her tragic act is irrevocably marked by an unsurmountable silence. Each explanation is not only belated but also imperfect and partial. It can be no more and no less than an addition – a refiguration, a commentary, an attempt at clarification, with the recognition of interpretive fallibility inevitably inscribed. Even if these missives do not offer us the key to the one locked chamber in the porous vault we have constructed around the life of Sylvia Plath, they do mark a new beginning. They leave us alone with our demand and our expectation that Ted Hughes might finally account for his part in their shared story. With these segments – written in anger and reproach, offering at times a sentimental transfiguration of the past, at times a rawly emotional rendition – he offers his last word in the case; a version which is unrelentlessly concerned with his release from the spell of death.

As the chairman of Faber & Faber explained upon publication of *Birthday Letters*, these poems indeed mark a birthday. Not the resurrection of a deceased poet, but rather the final closing of her open grave on the part of the mourner: 'When he finished writing them, or they finished with him, that was the moment to close that chapter in his life. And I do think he sees it as a chapter that is now over.' If for Ted Hughes these poems are meant to document that he has finally been able to control the demons that have haunted him since her death, for us their publication also suggests that Plath's writing can now perhaps not only be read apart from those who speak for her, who could never speak for herself. Rather, it can now also be read separated from our fantasy that someone holds the key to the crypt, given that the one most likely to do so has finally made his insight available to us. Some may fault Ted Hughes for not delivering what they expected – namely, that he would fill in the blanks in their marital crisis and above all shed light on the final weeks when she wrote not only her last poems but also the journal entries he destroyed. Others may counter that he has no obligation to do so. Instead, the publication of these poems reflect 'someone obsessed, stricken and deeply loving...always springing from a burning continuous present', as Andrew Motion puts it, 'a man remembering his young self, and the woman who overwhelmed him, in their full, flawed, utterly engrossing humanity'.[47] While A. Alvarez emphasizes their finality, judging 'they're complete in themselves and full of feeling, and the feeling seems wonderfully authentic', others criticize him, as does Elaine Showalter, for the 'very determinist view of her, that it was because of her father, and that she was doomed to die and there was nothing he could do to stop her'. Far more scathingly, Joyce Carol Oates maintains that this poetry 'lacks the originality and sharpness of Plath's poetry', which it mimics, only to continue by surmising: 'It's a testament to the power of what we might call contemporary biographical mania, that our interest in this capable, conventional poetry would only be stirred by our collective prurient interest in the poets' mismanaged lives.'[48] Again the question of literary merit is undecidable, ultimately coming down to aesthetic taste. At stake, instead, is that Ted Hughes has given us all he can, and the story he is willing to disclose is unequivocal. We can and should expect no more from him. The fact that the case for us is not closed is not his problem, but ours.

Writing on the question of transgenerational haunting, the French psychoanalysts Nicolas Abraham and Maria Torok define reality as a secret, a kernel of shared knowledge that has been rejected, masked, denied, buried, but preserved in a crypt within the psychic apparatus. Reality, comparable to an offence, a crime, they suggest, 'is born of the necessity of remaining concealed, unspoken'.[49] This reality as a past, this corpus of unspeakable words, which cannot quite die nor be fully revived, remains present in the subject, buried alive, unable to appear in the light of day yet, nevertheless, broadcasting its message to the afflicted subject, or to the next generation that has inherited this secret knowledge. Staying with the paradigm of burial sites and revenants, Abraham and Torok choose the notion of the phantom, a representation of a deceased come back to haunt the living with clandestine knowledge, as their critical trope for describing how, in the course of fantasy work, a given subject objectifies this gap in knowledge, owing to which a corpus of words remains unattainable while nevertheless also inhabiting a psychic topology of the subject. The analyst, they suggest, while called upon to put the unnameable into words, must take care not to destroy the psychic universe of the subject involved. The crypt not only preserves clandestine knowledge but also protects the subject's fantasy life by prohibiting any direct access to this cluster of words, which initially had such a disastrous impact on the subject that they had to be withdrawn from circulation. So as to resolve the dilemma of making an encrypted traumatic reality acceptable without translating it into yet another protective fantasy but also without inflicting upon the subject an unmitigated incursion of this disastrous knowledge, they offer as cure a prohibition against not telling. Undermining the prohibition against speech upon which the crypt is founded is meant to set a process in motion in the course of which the unutterable will change into a psychic representation, so that it can, in turn, be resolved.

Returning one last time to the issue of Sylvia Plath's grave, we could argue that, because her suicide poses a hermeneutic task even while it defies a conclusive solution to the questions her death raised about the origin of her multiple self-fashionings, her self-destructive drive, and her creative powers, at stake is the fact that her grave, whether marked or not, functions like a crypt in our cultural image repertoire. Sylvia Plath is buried alive in so far as her words draw their power from the way that they speak to us even while they preserve a secret. Something is not told, held back, and yet this corpus of unspeakable words also resiliently informs what we read by her. And, because we sense there is a secret to which we might find the key, we keep turning to those who speak for her, hoping to find the interpretation that will unlock the crypt. The troubling question is, of course, whether such a key can actually be found or whether it is irrevocably lost. Furthermore, even if we were to enter the crypt, would we really find the clandestine corpus intact, or would it not have disintegrated? The one certainty we have, however, is that a secret has been kept, because not only is something explicitly missing from the posthumous biographical representations. Rather, something has also implicitly been withheld by Sylvia Plath herself from her poetic and autobiographical texts, albeit unintentionally – a traumatic truth about herself in relation both to her family and to her history around which all her writing revolves, feeding upon it without directly touching it. By virtue of her so resiliently disparate textual traces, we can belatedly not only surmise the existence of a crypt, but also speculate that what we call a secret stands in for a knowledge of contingency so disastrous that it cannot directly be translated into a meaningful utterance about the luck or the misfortune of accident. In other words, any interpretative gesture that would transform this kernel of contingent knowledge into a coherent meaningful narrative about Sylvia Plath's fate inevitably means having recourse to the realm of representations, which are always approximations and transcriptions of the concealed reality but never the corpus of unspeakable words itself.

By advocating that we relinquish searching for a key and instead leave the crypt locked, I suggest shifting our discussion away from the question whether the Plath Estate is suppressing vital material or not, for it seems less fruitful for the project of literary interpretation to think of this guarded secret as a concrete corpus of unspeakable words that could, by virtue of analysis, be turned into a concrete fantasy scene, which could then in turn be resolved once and for all. Instead I suggest that, precisely because the traumatic knowledge has remained clandestine, we must not only recognize that the only materials available to us are the traces of this encrypted knowledge, coming belatedly as a result of the foreclosure. Rather we must also recognize that we can do nothing but respond to these textual representations with which Sylvia Plath came to articulate the questions that were so distressingly unresolvable to her – the burden of her gender, of her genealogy, and of the historical moment in which she came to formulate her desires and her discontent. The crypt of unspeakable words around which the body of her writing revolves, and whose most resilient manifestation is the game over who owns the facts of a dead poet's life, haunts us beyond any voyeuristic pleasure we might derive from seeking to find the truth of this case of the spectral Sylvia Plath speaking from beyond the grave. It does so, however, not in the sense of a universalizing narrative about how we all struggle against the burden of our past. Rather what continues to haunt us is her very particular refiguration of how disastrous knowledge is averted and yet also obliquely revealed.

Though it often does seem impossible to separate our reading of Sylvia Plath's texts from our fascination with the Plath myth, it does seem possible to separate her voice from those who have spoken for her in memoirs, biographies, and editorial commentary. My suggestion is that its distinctive tone can be discerned in the fault-lines that distinguish the many, often disparate voices in which she came to cast herself – the poems, the fictional texts, the autobiographical texts – as it is also articulated in the contradictions that emerge, as these texts, though emanating from one imagining subject, offer multiple representations of the same psychic reality. Reading all of her texts as the products of an incessant attempt at self-fashioning and thus accepting that the distinction between more or less autobiographical is no longer relevant, we liberate ourselves from the constrictive fantasy that there are facts to be uncovered. We leave the crypt intact and focus instead on its effects, for it is the haunting impact of the belated articulations we can share, not the secret.

2

The Autobiographical Writings

> Marilyn Monroe appeared to me last night in a dream as a kind of
> fairy godmother. An occasion of 'chattering' with audience much
> as the occasion with Eliot will turn out, I suppose. I spoke, almost
> in tears, of how much she and Arthur Miller meant to us, although
> they could, of course, not know us at all. She gave me an expert
> manicure. I had not washed my hair, and asked her about
> hairdressers, saying no matter where I went, they always imposed
> a horrid cut on me. She invited me to visit her during the
> Christmas holidays, promising a new flowering life.
>
> *(Jour.* Sunday, 4 October 1959)

Framing *The Journals of Sylvia Plath* with his foreword, Ted
Hughes suggests that, in contrast to all her other writings, these
texts represent 'her day to day struggle with her warring selves,
for herself only' *(Jour.* p. xv). Because of his conviction that all
her writing before *Ariel* was tainted by her ambition to produce
stories and poems in the manner required by the prestigious
magazines in which she wanted to see her work published,
Hughes locates the impulse behind this record of her psychic
strife in the 'relentless passion' as well as the 'fever of
uncertainty and self-doubt' with which she came 'to apprentice
herself to various masters and to adapt her writing potential to
practical, profitable use' *(Jour.* p. xiii). Enmeshed with this desire
for success, however, Hughes finds a second battle waged in the
pages of these *Journals.* As he confesses to the readers of these
autobiographical writings, 'Sylvia Plath was a person of many
masks, both in her personal life and in her writings. Some were
camouflage cliché facades, defensive mechanisms, involuntary.
And some were deliberate poses, attempts to find the keys to
one style or another.' Yet, while 'these were the visible faces of

her lesser selves, her false or provisional selves, the minor roles of her inner drama', the 'real self', Hughes surmises, was dumb for most of her life. Shut away beneath the bustle of 'conflicting voices of the false and petty selves', behind the 'bundles of contradictory and complementary selves' with which, like most people, she had come to present herself to the world, it only managed to find its voice in the *Ariel* poems. According to him, then, Sylvia Plath used her journals to record the process of psychic unmaking and remaking, the triumph of her real creative self over the bundle of contradictory, false selves. It is, of course, deeply ironical that he should have destroyed one and lost the other of precisely those two notebooks which contain entries for the last three years of her life, when, according to him, her voice would have been at its most real. Indeed, in a longer essay entitled 'Sylvia Plath and her Journals', Hughes admits that, looking over the curtailed journals, 'one cannot help wondering whether the lost entries for her last three years were not the more important section of it'. Given that the work that made her famous, the work he designates as her only real writing, was produced in those years, he recognizes 'we certainly have lost a valuable appendix to all that later writing'.[1]

Reading Ted Hughes's interpretative narrative against the grain, the spirit of contradiction begins to take hold. What if the voice of *Ariel* – though without doubt Plath's most powerful, astonishing poetic achievement – were no more real than the other voices? Which is to say, what if we were to relinquish privileging her final voice over the many conflicting voices that led up to the last three months of her life? Would that not allow us to discover a psychic truthfulness both in her lifelong ambition to be accepted by her peers against her sense of personal and cultural alienation, as well as in her obsession with fulfilling the expectations of those masters whose authority she had come to accept – notably her mother, her teachers, her husband, the editors of prestigious journals and publishing houses? At stake in renegotiating which is the voice of her true self, I contend, is not just a positive reappraisal of the body of writing she produced before her *Ariel* poems. Rather it would allow one to hear another story Plath's journal may well be telling us, not so much about a final triumphant remaking of the self as about the psychic cost involved in striving for a coherent and conclusive self, perfected after a long struggle with the contradictions and impasses posed by the contingencies of life. As Janet Malcolm notes, one could accuse Ted Hughes himself of producing what the market seemed to require, when he allowed the publication of both Sylvia Plath's *Letters Home* and *The Journals*. More significant, given that what is often remarkable about these curtailed editions is not what they leave out but what they let stand, she comes to regard Ted Hughes as 'a man trying to serve two masters and knowing that it isn't ever going to come out right' – on the one hand, the husband, 'seeking to disentangle his life from the Plath legend', on the other hand, the fellow literary artist, 'needlessly exposing himself to public scrutiny' so as to cultivate her posthumous reputation.[2] While the husband destroyed the journal she wrote with the one voice he felt was representative of his wife's real self ('the self I had married, after all, and lived with and knew well') because he 'did not want her children to have to read it' (*Jour.* pp. xiv-xi *passim*), the fellow artist makes public large portions of the preceding journals which, though seemingly speaking in the voice of false selves, compromise him along with all her other relatives and friends, though doing so obliquely.

One could speculate further whether this decision was motivated in part by the fellow artist sensing that the battle of her contradictory selves and not the Ariel-self speaking in unabashed anger constitutes the more profitable matrix for any belated reading of her poetic and narrative writings. Along these lines, Malcolm suggests that Plath used her journals to write 'about herself and the people she knew as if they were characters in a novel', so that we should read them as though they were 'a kind of furiously written first draft of a bildungsroman into which the writer pours everything, knowing there will be time later on to revise and cut and shape and order'.[3] Concerned with a biographic approach which does not seek as its authenticating point of reference a truth behind Sylvia Plath's plethora of voices but rather locates her authenticity in the mutually implicated transformations of the autobiographical and the literary voice, I will use this chapter to explore the complex and often incompatible versions of the artist as a young woman that she recorded in these journals, which, though written for herself only, nevertheless stage how these ambivalent self-fashionings came into being as the result of an imaginary dialogue with her various 'masters'. Not only does the young woman artist emerge as a knot of disparate selves, which Sylvia Plath tries out as she transforms the contingent material of her everyday life into a first, albeit unpolished narrative. This composite figure also proves to be performatively constructed. The so jarringly contradictory narrator of the journals comes into being as a result of responding to the cultural codes, social expectations, and aesthetic values embodied by the figures of authority for whose benefit, but also for whose recognition, Sylvia Plath undertook the complex process of self-fashioning in the first place. At issue in the exercises at self-fashioning recorded in these journals, I want to suggest, is whether the figure of the young woman artist fully recognizes herself in this interpellative call – that is, fully accepts the symbolic mandate provided by interpellation – or whether, resisting this identity, she comes to formulate a radical uncertainty about herself as the object of the predominant patriarchal symbolic order. In other words, what does questioning the very symbolic authority that she also appeals to entail for the construction of her subjectivity as a woman and as an artist?

My own reading is based on the premiss that *The Journals* represent Sylvia Plath's highly heterogeneous private archive of fantasy scenarios about herself and her relation to the world, which she came to revise, cut, shape, and order into more coherent versions – the letters addressed explicitly to her mother, in which, performing the part of the perfect daughter Sivvy, she offers an appeasing autobiographical novel, meant to satisfy her mother's expectations; *The Bell Jar*, addressed to a particular part of the literary market and written under a pseudonym, in which, performing the part of the discontented daughter Esther Greenwood, she offers a horrific autobiographical novel, in turn meant to frustrate the expectations of all interpellative maternal figures; finally the poems, where the lyrical I could fall back upon conventions of poetic form so as to offer a highly stylized refiguration of the crucial events of her psychic reality. In other words, I suggest seeing the disparate pieces of her writing – the early poems, the stories, the novel, the *Ariel* poems – as individual slices taken from the matrix of this journal transcription of psychic reality (written for and to herself) and reshaped into a secondary narrative, composed under the aegis of a given interpellator. As Janet Malcolm notes,

> Plath's relentlessly humourless vision of herself as the heroine of a great drama gives her journal a verve and a lustre that the journals of more restrained, self-deprecating, classical (as opposed to romantic) writers lack...Probably because Plath felt the chill of the void with such unnerving intensity did she need to put so many layers of heated self-absorption between herself and what lay outside.[4]

Yet at issue in these journals is the fact that they served Sylvia Plath as a record of her highly complex and inconsistent private theatre, with the plethora of self-fashionings defying not only the traumatic knowledge of psychic vulnerability haunting her but also defying any effort at constructing a unified version of herself. What also distinguishes *The Journals* is the way a presentation of conflicting descriptions of psychic reality is doubled by a narratorial voice commenting on this ambivalence, admonishing, reflecting, analysing only again to lose the upper hand. *The Journals* thus trace three distinct psychic registers – an onslaught of unmitigated spontaneous emotions, the imagination transforming this contingent material into pleasurable fantasy scenes about desire and rage, and the self-conscious critic evaluating the very psychic contradictions performed by this urge towards self-absorption. At stake, therefore, is not so much a battle between false and true versions of the self but rather an unresolvable scene of conflict. The critical self recognizes both the need for control and the fallibility of its powers; recognizes the need constantly to reposition itself in relation to the law of its chosen masters and the constraints responding to this interpellative call entails; recognizes the compelling force of fantasy for overcoming the self-doubt induced by scepticism and the fragile fictionality of any *mise-en-scène* of desire.

The first part of *The Journals*, containing entries from July 1950, when Sylvia Plath was about to begin her first year at Smith College, to July 1953, when in the course of a nervous breakdown she attempted suicide, begins with the statement, 'I may never be happy, but tonight I am content' (*Jour.* 3). The scenario she unfolds over the course of the next months is one of expectancy not uncommon to most young adults, who, having left the protection of a middle-class home for the first time, find themselves confronted with a range of possibilities from which to choose but also with an uncertainty about the outcome of this choice. Yet Sylvia, vacillating between sentimentality (praising the beauty of virginity, contemplating the transience of existence), nebulous sexual longing, fantasies about the ideal mate, and disgust at the conventions of dating, presents her frantic urge to find some meaning to her life as an antidote to a sense of panic, self-doubt, and madness inhabiting her psyche. The dilemma is, from the start, that of the sceptical subject, for, even while she feels an acute sense of estrangement from her fellow students at Smith, she recognizes that only social acceptance from her peers can allay her anxiety about being a 'faceless' non-entity; indeed a weekend date promises to be 'the only indication that I am a whole person, not merely a knot of nerves; without identity' (*Jour.* 17). While her extensive meditations on her loneliness in part lead to an enjoyment of melancholy that feeds upon fantasies of self-destruction ('you may as well dispose of the empty shell or present and commit suicide' (*Jour.* 18)), they in part also lead to a romantic elevation of her acute sense of being different from her peers as the necessary predicament of the young woman artist. Her state of troubled expectancy is, however, further heightened by an ambivalence about the very gift from which she seeks to gain self-certainty. While she assures herself 'I am justifying my life, my keen emotion, my feeling, by turning it into print' (*Jour.* 16), she also admits that, unable to tell her mother about her confusion over the sexual advances of a man, she recognizes that even this medium is fallible: 'After something happens to you, you go to write it down, and either you overdramatize it or underplay it, exaggerate the wrong parts or ignore the important ones. At any rate, you never write it quite the way you want to' (*Jour.* 5).

Fully aware that she longs for the recognition by another to assure herself of the integrity of her existence, she produces images of the perfect mate. Conceived in relation to her dependence and incompleteness, indeed as a response to her sense of vulnerability, she fantasizes the other as an ideal, who would, in turn, produce her as a perfected subject. Indeed, the

37

young woman artist Sylvia performs the psychic strategy Stanley Cavell calls the 'logic of scepticism', whereby the flawed subject imagines an ideal other, so that this other being might in turn conceive the sceptical subject in some sense in its own image of plenitude and infallibility.[5] At the same time, however, her longing for the perfect mate is also nourished by an acerbic analysis of what most American males find desirable in a woman. They worship woman 'as a sex machine with rounded breasts and a convenient opening in the vagina', she notes, 'as a painted doll who shouldn't have a thought in her pretty head other than cooking a steak dinner and comforting him in bed after a hard 9–5 day at a routine business job' (Jour. 22). At stake in her anguished meditations on loneliness is, then, the aporia that, even while her scepticism requires the recognition by another being to lend certainty and meaning to her existence, her refusal to subject herself to the predominant patriarchal symbolic laws makes her aware of the impossibility of her demand. Yet this resistance is likewise marked by psychic ambivalence, for, unwilling fully to accept a fixed gender position, she also recognizes her inability to escape this interpellative call entirely: 'I am at odds. I dislike being a girl, because as such I must come to realize that I cannot be a man. In other words, I must pour my energies through the direction and force of my mate. My only free act is choosing or refusing that mate. And yet, it is as I feared: I am becoming adjusted' (Jour. 23). Undecided in her choice between the constraint of adjusting to social norms in the manner her mother (her privileged representative of the symbolic law) advocates and a melancholic cultural alienation, which she sees as the prerequisite for her writing, she constructs an either/or scenario, in which significantly the gesture of undecidable scepticism is aligned with the fascination for self-destruction. The latter, furthermore, is as resilient a measure of certainty as her authorship and her desire for love and acceptance by another being: 'I have the choice of being constantly active and happy or introspectively passive and sad. Or I can go mad by ricocheting in between' (Jour. 24).

Two themes keep resurfacing in these deliberations. Embedded in her complaint about her culture's constrictive notion of proper feminine behaviour, which thwarts her desire for adventure and passionate sexual experiences and threatens to dull her powers of perception and articulation, she unfolds her ambivalent conception of the longed-for other being. Insisting 'it is only balance that I ask for. Not the continual subordination of one person's desires and interests to the continual advancement of another's' (*Jour*. 43), she also records her daydream of being 'raped in a huge lust like a cave woman, fighting, screaming, biting in a ferocious ecstasy of orgasm' (*Jour*. 73), even while she notes that the mate she is conceiving for herself is in danger of turning into 'a demigod of a man' (*Jour*. 78). Duplicating her inability to fashion herself outside the very codes of femininity she also finds so limiting, we find a similar dilemma in relation to her writing, which in her most critical mode she finds 'too much clinging to clichés and downtrodden combinations. Not enough originality. Too much blind worship of modern poets and not enough analysis and practice' (*Jour*. 32). Ultimately both the mating problem and the writing problem merge in a deliberation on the 'basic and egoistic self-love' that is coterminous with her self-doubt. Recognizing her envy of the way men have the freedom to have a career, a sexual and a family life, she also notes: 'I am vain and proud. I will not submit to having my life fingered by my husband, enclosed in the larger circle of his activity, and nourished vicariously by tales of his actual exploits' (*Jour*. 35). Thus not the love for another but rather writing itself is conceived as that which gives certainty to her existence: 'it is as necessary for the survival of my haughty sanity as bread is to my flesh' (*Jour*. 37). And yet self-love inevitably ricochets back as self-doubt. Ultimately she cannot decide whether her sense of being different, of rejecting the cultural values imposed on her, is proof of her existence in the sense that it offers her the security that she is, in essence, a poet, or whether her writing is merely a cover for her social failure, not essential to her being but simply one of several choices open to her, like marriage and maternity. In the course of these deliberations, every effort at replenishing her self-love by projecting a perfect mate, social and academic success, and perfectionism in writing is followed by the fear that all of these ambitions are highly precarious protective fictions – arbitrary, exchangeable, and transient.

The scenario of psychic expectation so prevalent in the first part of *The Journals* thus traces the same trajectory. While melancholia emerges from self-doubt, an egoistic self-love is recuperated by virtue of an intellectual balancing of choices and in turn introduces moments of manic self-exaltation, which, however, transform back into depression once the choices reality poses are recognized as contradictory and undecidable: 'I want to kill myself, to escape from responsibility, to crawl back abjectly into the womb. I do not know who I am, where I am going' (*Jour.* 59). In the midst of her melancholic self-doubt she is able to conceive of her identity only as a response to the expectations of others – be this the conception of public success, of the ideal mate, or of her gift as an author – even while she recognizes that this safeguard against self-destruction is fragile. Such ambivalent resistance to the interpellative call, around which her scenario of scepticism revolves, is, furthermore, rhetorically underlined in those passages where the narrator Sylvia abandons the first-person singular she uses to record her pride at her academic successes, her fear that she has not fulfilled the expectations others have invested in her, her doubt at the stability of her ambitions, and her invocation of mortality as the one certainty of her existence. Splitting herself into subject and object of interpellation, she takes on the role of stern observer: 'Face it kid, you've had a hell of a lot of good breaks' (*Jour.* 53). In other words, the scenario of psychic expectation played through in these first journal entries incessantly shifts back and forth between various voices. The egotistically self-absorbed Sylvia articulates her inability to deal with incoherence ('my life up till now seems messy, inconclusive, disorganized'), indulges in her own failure ('I am drowning in negativism, self-hate, doubt, madness'), and ridicules her ambition to live a diversity of lives ('I am a conglomerate garbage heap of loose ends' (*Jour.* 60)). The harsh critic Sylvia in turn appeals to the power of intellectual self-control over a self-indulgence, whose reference is either unblighted happiness or self-annihilation. Reminding herself 'you are twenty. You are not dead, although you were dead,' she admonishes herself to 'let there be continuity at least – a core of consistency – even if your philosophy must be always a moving dynamic dialectic'. Finally, the author Sylvia who is already transforming the Sylvia afflicted with self-doubt into the protagonist of her autobiographical speculation, narrates her bouts of melancholic anguish as though she were speaking from the position of one of her interpellated masters: 'I have gone through my winter solstice, and the dying god of life and fertility is reborn.... I am glad I wrote some of the sick naked hell I went through down in here. Otherwise, from my present vantage point, I could hardly believe it' (*Jour.* 69). And yet, to find a synthesis between projecting a fully integrated self, freed of all doubt, on the one hand, and, on the other, embarking on fantasies of suicide, involves transforming the egoistic demand – namely, that one's existence be either fully intact or nothing – into accepting incompatible desires. It would require acknowledging that her desire for coherence, articulated in her wish to 'order life in sonnets and sestinas' is fundamentally enmeshed with an acceptance of contingency: 'there is no security, no artifice to stop the uncanny changes, the rat race, the death unwish' (*Jour.* 79). Even as Sylvia conceives of the integrity of her existence to be dependent on the love of another ('I want so obviously, so desperately to be loved, and to be capable of love' (*Jour.* 69)), she also recognizes that 'love is a desperate artifice to take the place of those two original parents who turned out not to be omnisciently right gods' (*Jour.* 79). At the same time she holds onto this very artifice as her one apotropaic charm against the troubling knowledge of parental fallibility: 'love is an illusion, but I would willingly fall for it if I could believe in it' (*Jour.* 79).

These first journal entries culminate, however, in a performance of the psychic impasse which proved from the start to be so fundamental to her fantasy scenario of expectancy and self-doubt. As her negotiation of disparate narratives about love, success, and aesthetic accomplishment proves unsatisfactory, she falls back on either denying herself all articulation of discontent or fully embracing the other narrative subtending her psychic reality – namely, her fascination with suicide. The last two entries record the voice of the critic, ridiculing her ('you are an inconsistent and very frightened hypocrite...right now you are sick in your head'), chastising her ('you have gone the limit...You saw visions of yourself in a straight jacket, and a drain on the family, murdering your mother in actuality, killing the edifice of love and respect built up over the years in the hearts of other people') and seeking to impose the law of survival ('Where are you? I want you, need you: the belief in you and love and mankind. You must not seek escape like this, you must think,' (*Jour.* 86))). Yet the editorial comment immediately following upon this command, stating that 'Journals have disappeared – if they existed – for the two years after Plath's breakdown in the summer of 1953' only serves to heighten the sense one has of the mutual implication between this radical self-interpellation and the truncated voice of her first suicide attempt. What is striking about the entries with which her first set of journals ends is the way Sylvia both indulges in self-pity and belittles her anguish, taking on simultaneously the role of victim, torturer, and analyst in this fantasy scenario of self-doubt and guilt. We sense that a crime has been committed, for which she must pay, and yet its nature remains secret. All we hear, on the one hand, is the voice of melancholia, tormenting her by articulating an irrecuperable traumatic loss, which invokes in her a desire for her own self-destruction, and, on the other, the voice of the critic, punishing her for her falliblities, which in turn invokes a sense of guilt about the fact that she is not mastering the task of survival, not fitting in, leaving something wanting.

The second part of *The Journals* opens with Sylvia Plath a promising American student in Cambridge. While the entries prior to her suicide invoke the family in relation to a question of loss, with Sylvia casting herself as a psychic orphan, having no home to return to, unable to communicate properly with her mother, unwilling to accept her mother's notion of happiness, these entries rework the scenario of scepticism in relation to an idealized lost father, on the one hand, who supports the nostalgic fantasy that a lost state of plenitude can be regained, and, on the other hand, a stoic mother, representing the reality principle of survival in the face of a lack in plenitude. Casting herself as Lazarus, Sylvia declares, 'that story has such a fascination. Being dead I rose up again...coming out of the grave with the scars and the marring mark on my cheek which (is it my imagination?) grows more prominent' (*Jour.* 100). This sense of having returned to the living, of needing to find a new home, is coupled with an appeal to different surrogate figures of parental authority, to whom she can address her desire for certainty. The first to appear is her psychiatrist, of whom she says, 'I feel I need him. I need a father. I need a mother' (*Jour.* 100) and whom she apostrophizes at the onset of one of her most riveting descriptions of melancholy, where an over-identification with the image of the successful, accomplished daughter transforms into self-hatred: 'Dear Doctor...Hostility grows. That dangerous, deadly venom which comes from a sick heart. Sick mind, too. The image of identity we must daily fight to impress on the neutral, or hostile, world, collapses inward; we feel crushed' (*Jour.* 104). As in the earlier entries, an admission of self-hatred and loss of psychic anchorage is seen as the result of 'foundering in relativity'. Whenever she finds that her world – men, writing, her girl friends, academic life – fails to reassure her of a consistency in being, all her striving for success appears to be nothing but 'hectic activity to cover up the fear that must face itself and duel itself to death' (*Jour.* 106). Invoking the resilient courage of her mother, who, as paragon of survival, had so successfully rebuilt her family after the loss of her husband, is in turn meant to lead her away from the fatal scenario of 'either all or nothing' and towards the 'intermediate path of meaningful activity' (*Jour.* 106), towards living 'the golden mean' (*Jour.* 116). The familial configuration she conceives as validation of her consistency in being thus positions her between a figure of paternal authority (the psychiatrist) to whom she appeals for comfort and a maternal figure whom she imitates in her stoic attitude of survival. And, as in the earlier entries, at stake in this strategy of self-reassurance is the way her sense of social alienation (not getting published, not finding a mate) is inextricably enmeshed with her fear of 'the death of the imagination' (*Jour.* 110). The troubling point, however, is not just that one stands in for the other: 'I justified the mess I made of life by saying I'd give it order, form, beauty, writing about it; I justified my writing by saying it would be published, give me life (and prestige to life)' (*Jour.* 110). Rather both are also negotiated in relation to the traumatic sense of a loss, subtending all the self-fashionings she engages in – be these the texts she writes or the personal narratives of academic and marital success she wishes to live. That this indulgence in melancholy is, however, as much a self-fashioning as her enjoyment of ambition suggests itself by virtue of the fact that, once each individual crisis has passed, she cultivates a splendid indifference towards her anguish, and is able once again to 'marshal a stiff squadron of optimism, and trek' (*Jour.* 107).

Into this scenario of scepticism Sylvia suddenly, and indeed rather dramatically, introduces Ted Hughes, perhaps her most privileged interpellator, in an entry she entitles 'a small note after a large orgy' (*Jour.* 111).[6] Yet it is not merely the violence of the encounter that is striking 'I was stamping and he was stamping on the floor, and then he kissed me bang smash on the mouth [...]...And when he kissed my neck I bit him long and hard on the cheek, and when we came out of the room, blood was running down his face. [...] And I screamed in myself, thinking: oh, to give myself crashing, fighting, to you' (*Jour.* 113). Rather, in this narrative rendition, the 'big dark hunky boy, the only one here huge enough for me' (*Jour.* 122) emerges in the guise of what Abraham and Torok call a psychic phantom – a representation of a deceased conjured up in someone's psychic reality so as to objectify a gap in knowledge.[7] Even while she is still waiting for Ted to prove himself as the ideal mate she has so desperately been waiting for, she merges this longing with her desire for the lost father. In her complaint about not getting the lover she wants, she apostrophizes him, as prototype for the situation of abandonment ('Father, it hurts, oh, Father I have never known; a father, even, they took from me' (*Jour.* 124)), only to refigure her sexual dissatisfaction into a scene of incest ('My villanelle was to my father [...] I lust for the knowing of him' (*Jour.* 129)) where writing and sexual desire blur completely. At the same time, Sylvia, who designates herself throughout *The Journals* as a manic-depressive hysteric, falls back on the histrionic exaggeration so typical for this psychosomatic disorder, which physicians in the nineteenth century had come to describe as 'mythomania' and 'much ado about nothing'.[8] Transforming her encounter with Ted Hughes into a patchwork of mythic love stories, she calls out in the voice of a post-war Juliet: 'Please let him come; let me have him for this British spring...Please let him come, and give me the resilience & guts to make him respect me, be interested, and not to throw myself at him with loudness or hysterical yelling; calmly, gently, easy, baby, easy'. Plath conforms to another aspect of hysterical language, precisely not the display of uncontrolled emotions and body gestures but rather the protean ability to shift from one role to the next, while demonstrating a *belle indifférence* to all abandoned roles. She transforms the prior passionate attitude of desperate longing into that of controlled patience: 'And I sit, spider like, waiting, here, home; Penelope weaving webs of Webster, turning spindles of Tourneur' (*Jour*. 131). And also fully in line with the way the psychosomatic articulations of the hysteric not only give voice to the fact that reminiscences have not been successfully abreacted, but do so in a psychic gesture that points to an over-abundance of fantasy work, Sylvia's merging of the image of the dead father she has refused to relinquish with that of the long-awaited lover points to the way the recuperation of loss, the triumph over a sense of loneliness and abandonment, articulates a real desire, but does so as a formation of fantasy, which is to say as one of many scenarios that could be abandoned with the same fervour that it had initially come to be embraced.

Indeed, as a phantomatic refiguration of the dead father, Ted inspires not only the sense of self-certainty but also the fascination for self-destruction. As Sylvia once more abandons the role of the waiting lover for the more active one of whore, going to meet her desired mate, she casts him in the role of a dark nocturnal marauder to whom she can play the hungry slut: 'sick. With this desperate fury... love turns, lust turns, into the death urge' (*Jour*. 133).[9] The so resiliently protean language of hysteria finally allows her not only to displace her sexual lust and her death urge onto a surrogate figure for the lost father but, more importantly, to design for herself a fulfilment of the family romance, which the early death of her father had transformed into a nostalgic tale of lost plenitude and intactness. Upon hearing that Ted's book of poems *The Hawk and the Rain* has won a prize, she declares, 'together, we are the most faithful, creative, healthy simple couple imaginable', and projects her fantasy: 'We will publish a bookshelf of books between us before we perish! And a batch of brilliant healthy children' (*Jour*. 154). As a phantasmatic refiguration of the infallible father she has encrypted in her psyche, Ted serves as the other being around whom she can spin a counter-narrative to the one of self-doubt and egotistical self-love, in the course of which she gains proof of her own existence by virtue of being produced in the image of the other being whom she has conceived as perfect, as the answer to her sense of dependence and incompleteness. As she fashions their relation into a scenario of restoration, putting closure on the horrors and fears that began when her father died, she conceives for herself a new dependence, in which the life of the other is the stake for her own existence: 'I get quite appalled when I realize...my whole being has grown and interwound so completely with Ted's that if anything were to happen to him, I do not see how I could live' (*Jour.* 156). In the role of the daughter, dependent on another's knowledge, oblivious to her prior refusal to have a husband fully controlling her life, she now conceives of Ted both as a mentor in learning to master survival – 'I live in him until I live on my own' (*Jour.* 185) – and as a teacher in learning to master her poetic gift, accepting the exercises he sets her to reawaken her dormant imagination. As in the earlier part of *The Journals*, writing and living merge, only now the scenario of self-doubt has transformed into one of mutual reassurance: 'My life is discipline...I live for my own work, without which I am nothing. My writing. Nothing matters but Ted, Ted's writing and my writing' (*Jour.* 204).

Yet even while, in an entry she writes on Mother's Day, 11 May 1958, Sylvia explicitly designates her father as 'the buried male muse and god-creator risen to be my mate in Ted' (*Jour.* 222), under the auspices of a quarrel this idealized lover suddenly transforms into a figure of threat, of whom she notes, 'if he weren't my husband I would have run from him as a killer' (*Jour.* 219), only to transform once more into the guarantor of domestic normality, when, waking from nocturnal visions of sickness and death, she perceives him as 'Ted, my saviour, emerging out of the néant with a tall mug of hot coffee' (*Jour.* 220). Indeed, her unbroken dependence on her perfect mate lets her fall prey to jealousy, envy, anger, humiliation, and burning loneliness when her trust in him is called into question, even while his existence is also the guarantee of her self-certainty: 'steady on. I have my one man' (*Jour.* 188). Indeed, Ted proves to be not simply the perfect other, saving her from her psychic demons, nor in a darker mode the figure of sexual violence, but rather also a representative of the public law, whose harsh interpellation she interprets both as a stifling and an invigorating call for success. Even while Sylvia nourishes the fantasy of perfect domestic bliss, she continues to indulge in her psychic deliberations, in the course of which she holds before her eyes 'the gulf between my desire & ambition and my naked abilities' (*Jour.* 155), taunts herself for not being able to write or think, only to shift moods completely and exalt in manically overestimating her own poetic gift: 'I think I have written lines which qualify me to be The Poetess of America (as Ted will be The Poet of England and her dominions)' (*Jour.* 211). But, because her murderous 'demon self' – which repeatedly disrupts her fantasies of plenitude by demanding she accept nothing less than perfection and punishes her with guilt when she shows signs of fallibility – speaks the voice of precisely the social interpellation which punishes and sustains her, Ted emerges not as its antidote but rather as its ally. In much the same manner that she seeks to hide her fallibilities from her mother, whom she conceives as her privileged figure of the call for survival, she cultivates duplicity towards Ted. Although his perfection is meant to assuage her self-doubt, it actually nourishes the relentless harsh self-critic inhabiting her with a murderous law that allows only perfection: 'keep quiet with Ted about worries. With him around, I am disastrously tempted to complain, to share fears and miseries... But my fears are only magnified when reflected by him' (*Jour.* 179).

The second part of *The Journals* ends with a fantasy scenario of jealous rage, which on the thematic level illustrates how the scene of scepticism can inspire a sudden shift from the completeness of love to the perfection of doubt even while on the narrative level it demonstrates some of Plath's best qualities as an author of fiction (*Jour.* 227–36 *passim*). The scene is framed by a description of how Sylvia, once she loses her unconditional faith in the other, succumbs to paranoid jealousy and is overcome with self-disgust at having endowed another being with unconditional trust. Spurred on by tales she has heard from an older male colleague about the dangers of Smith students, she begins to fantasize about adultery while listening to Ted read the part of Creon during a performance of *Oedipus*, which he had asked her not to attend. In the mode of the sceptic, she is only too willing to interpret his prohibition as the sign of some secret misdemeanour ('he was ashamed of something'), so that, scrutinizing him for further signs to support her sudden doubt, his face appears as a 'mean wrong face'. With the scene of jealousy prepared by this episode, she proceeds to describe the events of the following day. For her last day of teaching at Smith, she has, significantly, prepared texts about the 'joy of revenge, the dangerous luxury of hate and malice, and how, even when malice and venom are "richly deserved", the indulgence of these emotions can, alas, be ruinous'. Having time to spare before her classes begin, she goes alone to a coffee shop only to find Bill Van Voris, who during the reading the night before had been 'luxuriating over the words: loins, incest, bed, foul', speaking with a female student. This sight further fuels her fantasy about adultery – 'students made mistresses. Students made wives' – and as images of betrayal pile up she even imagines the death of her colleague's wife, Jacky. Having asked Ted to pick her up at the end of her classes so that they might celebrate the beginning of her freedom from the constraints of academia, she is astonished not to find him waiting for her in the parking lot, and, after not finding him in the library either, finally feels fully confirmed in her belief in his infidelity.

Upon leaving this arsenal of all the mythic texts that have so over-abundantly taken hold of her hysteric imagination, she finally sites him, though significantly as a phantom: 'I had one of those intuitive visions. I knew what I would see, what I would of necessity meet, and I have known for a very long time, although not sure of the place or date of the first confrontation'. In contrast to the predominant image of Ted as a resurrection of the nostalgic image of the father who promises plenitude, he now stands in for the paternal figure who did not come through, who abandoned and disappointed her trust. What she suddenly detects is the 'broad, intense smile' with which he seems to respond to 'the uplifted doe-eyes of a strange girl with brownish hair, a large lipsticked grin, and bare thick legs in khaki Bermuda shorts'. Placing this image, which she sees 'in several sharp flashes, like blows' next to that of Van Voris in the coffee shop, she interprets this as but one of many treacheries, indeed nothing but the final confirmation of all the doubt that has been haunting her: 'The late comings home, my vision, while brushing my hair, of a black-horned, grinning wolf all came clear, fused, and I gagged at what I saw'. As jealousy turns into disgust, she moves from the fantasy of suicide to that of the abused wife, bereft of all faith, who after a long period of trusting blindness sees 'too clearly'. In the voice of Othello, she chastises herself for having loved too sincerely and locates her 'ironic and fatal step' in having trusted that Ted 'was unlike other vain and obfuscating and self-indulgent men'. Having once again returned to the psychic rhetoric so prevalent to her deliberations, demanding either all or nothing, over-abundance of love transforms into total lack of love. For her, certainty can be gained only by merging completely with the other or by insisting that 'love is a lie and all joyous sacrifice is ugly duty', not, however, as the golden mean her mother so adamantly recommends.

The next entry, written almost a month later, is composed under the auspices of self-conscious guilt: 'I have avoided writing here because of the rough and nightmarish entry I must take up from – but I take up and knit up the raveled ends.' Noting only the traces of the violence that the couple had inflicted upon each other at the height of their dispute – her sprained thumb and his bloody claw marks – she assures herself: 'Air cleared. We are intact. . . . nothing is worth jeopardizing what I have'. As though to commemorate this restored trust, Sylvia concludes her fantasies about their future as a successful writing couple, however, by describing a twilight scene as violent as that preceding it, only now the violence has been deflected onto those who had initially inspired her jealousy – the sexually dangerous female college students. About to take a walk in the park next to their home, she decides to take 'a pair of silver-plated scissors in my raincoat pocket with the intent to cut another rose,' which, meant as a metaphor for their restored reunion, she hopes to watch bud. Yet, just as Sylvia is about to snip a pink bud, she is disturbed by a cackling sound and the sight of three hulking girls coming out of the rhododendron grove.'[10] Once they have walked away, she finds a rare orange rosebud, clips it, and, with this stolen treasure in hand, the blissful couple enters the grove, the site of clandestine sexual behaviour, only to discover newspapers loaded with scarlet and bright pink rhododendrons. The anger Sylvia had invoked against men, as she had watched Ted 'coming up the road from Paradise Pond, where girls take their boys to neck on weekends' is now aimed at the three girls, who, having returned, are forcefully reprimanded for having picked all the flowers. Finally, however, the couple, standing in the rain, with lightning flashing 'almost clear red' watches helplessly as the girls load the bunches of rhododendrons into the trunk of their car. Yet the narrator ends not on the note of resignation, but rather contemplating her own 'split morality'. Not just is she fully cognisant of the way the proper woman, who clips a single rose so as to watch it bud in her living room, is simply the restrained version of her murderous impulses. Indeed, the last sentences of the narrative laud her own destructive powers, that far outmatch those of the younger girls, clandestinely picking bunches of rhododendron for a dance: 'I have a violence in me that is hot as death-blood. I can kill myself or – I know it now – even kill another... I gritted to control my hands, but had a flash of bloody stars in my head as I stared that sassy girl down, and a blood-longing to [rush] at her and tear her to bloody beating bits.' Equally crucial is the way her self-fashioning as a murderess points to the violence which, though screened out, subtends her family romance with Ted, a murderous impulse that requires a scapegoat if the sceptic's completeness of love is to be preserved against a perfection of doubt.

The third part of *The Journals* covers her time as a freelance writer in Boston and finally her return to England. While the second part circles primarily around Ted as a phantom refiguration of the lost father, this last part involves jettisoning her diverse masters, vacillating between a 'desire for dependency & feeling it is wrong to be dependant' (*Jour*. 289). While Sylvia continues to chart both her ambitions and successes as well as her hysteria (whose symptoms are sickness, frenzy of resentment, insomnia, exhaustion, destructive paralysis, ruinous brooding, and daydreaming), she also begins to convince herself that, having become 'too dependent on Ted,' she must reject the very person whose interpellative call had previously promised certainty in the midst of self-doubt. Perceiving his orders no longer as supportive of her poetic gift but rather as marked by a stifling fanaticism, she admonishes herself: 'I must be myself – make myself and not let myself be made by him' (*Jour*. 245). At the same time she also begins to question whether placing her trust in public recognition is, indeed, a dependable guarantee for her poetic gift. The continual fear and paralysis that, along with her destructive rationalizing, prohibits her from writing, induces doubt whether she is truly a writer or whether she has merely been 'living in an idle dream of *being a writer,*' sustained by her early successes with *Seventeen* and *Mademoiselle.* What makes these anguished deliberations both so irritating and so compelling is that, conforming to the language of hysteria, Sylvia not only resiliently produces ever new debilitating symptoms but equally resiliently abandons them again, so that the paralysis and panic are shown to depart as miraculously as they come. Indeed, comparable to some of the cases Sigmund Freud and Josef Breuer discussed in their *Studies on Hysteria,* after each onslaught of a bout of hysteric incapacitation, Sylvia comments on such scenes in the voice of the critic, sensing that her absolute and obliterating panic was an oblique articulation of a desire for which she cannot directly find words: 'I have been ridiculously exhausted every morning, as if waking out of a coma, a queer deathlike state...what is it? I am in the prime of life, my best years ahead to work in, to write poems and have children, and I am exhausted' (*Jour.* 252).

Furthermore, in tandem with her desire to draw a clearer boundary between herself and her husband – 'The first thing is the early rising. Also, telling Ted nothing' (*Jour.* 286) – she begins a similar renegotiation of trust in her mother: 'must keep clear of any confiding in Mother' (*Jour.* 260). Privileging instead the interpellative call of her new therapist, Sylvia once again returns to the fantasy scenario of matricide, which had possessed her just before her first suicide attempt. Exploring her complex hostility for her mother, Sylvia gives voice not only to the guilt she feels because her mother had sacrificed everything for her children, but also her anger over the fact that, by marrying an older man, her mother was herself in part guilty for the premature loss of her husband. Yet, if expressing this hostility helps free Sylvia 'from the Panic Bird on my heart and my typewriter' (*Jour.* 266), it does so in part because it leads her to question maternal interpellation in general: 'all the mothers? What to do when you feel guilty for not doing what they say, because, after all, they have gone out of their way to help you?' (*Jour.* 270). She thus finds herself caught in the hysteric's indecision of whether to conceive of herself in relation to a symbolic mandate that is both constrictive and sustaining, or whether to break free entirely from all external expectations at the cost, however, of losing all symbolic identity in the process.

51

In other words, her hysteric incapacitation could be read as an oblique articulation of the fact that, for her, authorship is inextricably enmeshed with the very paralysing panic that also kept getting in the way of her writing, as though indulging in these scenarios of hostility towards others as well as towards herself was the screen for an unspeakable body of encrypted traumatic knowledge haunting her, feeding her self-deliberations, propelling her towards ever new self-figurations.

Through the end of these published *Journals* Ted continues to be cast as a repetition of the lost father, a male muse she both admires and shuns, yet in relation to whom trust is precariously transformed into the anxiety about being abandoned. In so far as Sylvia also keeps refiguring the child's jealousy of the mother, this desired maternal position is occupied by that of Lady Death, not just, however, in the sense that her beloved father preferred her to his daughter. Rather the maternal figure is cast as the muse for her suicide, which she calls 'a transferred murderous impulse from my mother onto myself' (*Jour.* 279). At the same time, even though on the thematic level she nostalgically invokes the male muse as a trope for lost plenitude, it is significantly the maternal interpellative call to whom her authorship concretely responds. Exploring what the mature thing to do 'with hostility for mother' might be, she recognizes that it is ultimately her highly ambivalent conception of maternal desire which paralyses her. According to her fantasy scenario, not writing allows her to punish and to satisfy her mother in one and the same gesture. Because while, on the one hand, this failure frustrates her mother's aspirations for her daughter's fame, it validates her insistence that privileging the life of a freelance writer over all other forms of employment threatens her daughter's financial security. Thus, regardless of whether Sylvia conceives of her mother, who had given up her desire to become an author when she married, as appropriating her daughter's writing so as to turn her into an extension of the self she could not develop, or whether she posits her writing as a substitute for herself, which her mother can love in her stead – 'if you don't love me, love my writing and love me for my writing' – in either case at issue is a negotiation of this maternal bond (*Jour.* 279–81 *passim*). As the inspiration behind her 'phantom of competition, the ego-centre of self-consciousness'

(*Jour*. 315) it is significantly the maternal figure who, in contrast to the lost father, stands both for survival and for the curtailment public recognition entails. Indeed, Sylvia recognizes that, in the course of her refiguration of the family romance into a lost father, promising narcissistic plenitude, and a castrative mother, promising success but with it the perpetual fear of being found wanting, she has dissipated her mother's image and transformed her into 'all editors and publishers and critics and the World, and I want acceptance there, and to feel my work good and well-taken. Which ironically freezes me at my work, corrupts my nunnish labor of work-for-itself-as-its-own-reward' (*Jour*. 303). Against the harsh maternal figure, so relentlessly representing symbolic law, she pits fantasies about her own maternity ('I want to be an Earth Mother' (*Jour*. 310)), and yet her blackly hysterical melancholia keeps reverting back into psychic impasse. For the young woman writer, not yet 30, authorship emerges as the unresolvable dilemma between defining herself only in relation to others ('passive dependence: on Ted, on people around me' (*Jour*. 325)) and liberating herself from the constraints of public expectation ('forget about audience' (*Jour*. 321)); letting go of self-absorption ('I shall perish if I can write about no one but myself' (*Jour*. 325)), and conceding that, in so far as her writing is 'a way of ordering and reordering the chaos of experience' (*Jour*. 281), it can never be severed from the psychic panic that paralyses and prohibits the very act of self-articulation it also nourishes.

In Sylvia Plath's autobiographic portrait of her struggles as a young woman artist, the psychic impasse of scepticism translates uncannily into the hysteric's concern with keeping the question of identity undecided, oscillating between various self-fashionings, celebrating each, but as constructions. As Jacques Lacan argues in his discussion of Freud's case study on Dora, the hysteric places herself in relation to a figure of paternal authority, sustaining his desire even as she ceaselessly questions the authority of his power.[11] But the hysteric's position before this symbolic law is also contradictory, given that, although she accepts that the question of her existence can be articulated only in relation to symbolic interpellation, she, nevertheless, perpetually renegotiates her relation to the

53

expectations she is asked to fulfil. This exchange, crossing the issue of sexual designation with that of contingency in being, revolves, on the one hand, around the question 'Am I a man or a woman?' and, on the other, 'Am I or might I not be?' Precisely the enmeshment of these two paradigms, Lacan notes in another article, 'conjugates the mystery of the hysterical subject's existence, binding it in the symbols of procreation and death'.[12] Thus the question of her existence, repeatedly performed in relation to a privileged figure of symbolic authority, will bathe the hysteric, support her, invade her, tear her apart, and this psychic deliberation is what the various psychosomatic symptoms of the hysteric come to articulate. Yet particularly striking about the young artist Sylvia, whose contradictory self-fashionings find such compelling articulation in the pages of *The Journals*, is not only the way she uses the hysteric's question – 'Am I male or female?, am I or am I not?' – so as to negotiate which social identity seems most viable to her. Rather this undecidability turns upon a crisis in imagination. As she keeps deliberating – 'Am I an artist or not?' and 'How do I align my desire for public recognition with my authorship?' – doubting the stability of any one role readily shifts into doubting the essentiality of her writing, so that both her social identity and her authorship veer towards a void.

In so doing, however, she actually touches upon the question which, according to Slavoj Zizek, lies at the heart of the hysteric mode of communication – namely, whether one believes that, beyond one's symbolic mandate there is inside one some substantial kernel, some hidden treasure which constitutes one's being, or whether one believes that there is nothing beneath the various assumed roles. The hysteric subject, he suggests, knows about the void around which all symbolic constructions of the self revolve, indeed seeks to preserve this 'nothing', which is why her protest against the master's interpellation is so ambivalent. The hysteric subject, acknowledging and at the same time shielding herself from the traumatic knowledge of a void at the navel of all self-constructions, needs her masters and cannot do without them, so there is never a simple and direct way out of her psychic dilemma. Zizek suggests formulating the vicious circle performed by the language of hysteric desire as follows: 'I, the subject, never know what I really want, since the Other's desire remains forever an enigma to me.'[13] From this he deduces that hysteria should be seen both as 'a failed interpellation, a rejection of the identity imposed on the subject by the predominant form of interpellation, a questioning of this identity' and as the articulation of 'the radical, constitutive uncertainty as to what, as an object, I am for the other'.[14]

Read in conjunction with the portrait of a young woman artist that emerges from the journal entries, the *Letters Home* document precisely the way hysteria performs a crisis in interpellation. If in *The Journals* Sylvia Plath appropriates both the voice of the agonized poet, isolated and tormented, as well as that of the critical tormentor to whom all self-doubt is addressed, the Sivvy of the letters is constructed quite explicitly in response to her mother's interpellative call. Yet the terrible disparity that emerges when one reads these letters in tandem with the journal entries forces one to realize how they are haunted by a secret. Not only are all the anguished psychic deliberations left unspoken in these letters, but, equally important, her rejection of her mother's stoic optimism, her inability fully to recognize herself in this call for survival, is equally suppressed. While in the journals, written to herself, she indulges in a description of her social alienation and loss of identity, in the letters, written to her mother, she indulges in her assertions of successful assimilation. On 28 September 1950 she writes: 'We had our college assembly this morning. I never came so close to crying since I've been here when I saw the professors, resplendent with colors, medals, and emblems, march across the stage and heard adorable Mr. Wright's stimulating address. I still can't believe I'm a SMITH GIRL!...The whole house is just the friendliest conglomeration of people imaginable' (*LH* 46). Yet it would be too simple to say that the letters deny all sense of social and emotional discontent. Rather at stake is the way Sylvia Plath colours the events and shapes herself differently depending on the addressee of her writing, so that perhaps an authenticity of voice can be located precisely at the faultline between the melancholic scepticism of *The Journals* and the 'old resilient optimism' (*LH* 59) of the *Letters Home*. Furthermore, the buoyancy Sivvy exhibits in these letters draws its strength precisely from the fact that her depressions need not be named directly, since, implicitly, this is the secret subtending her ambitions, which she shares with her mother. Even while she proudly relates her successes and joys to her mother, involves her in any plans she makes about her future profession, and interprets the money she earns through prizes as a financial relief for her mother, she also admits feeling homesick, insecure, and uncertain in the unfamiliar environment of college, and writes endlessly about the poems that have been rejected. In other words, at issue is not so much that Sivvy can perform her buoyant self only by virtue of censoring material in these letters, but rather that, identifying with the resilient optimism her mother expects from her, she can control her psychic demons. Appealing to her mother as an apotropaic charm against self-doubt and destructive self-indulgence, she pleads, 'Do write me letters, Mommy, because I am in a very dangerous state of feeling sorry for myself' (*LH* 88). She does mention her psychic disarray and her sense of utter fatigue, brought on by one of her sinus infections ('I am mentally so disorganized that I can't retain knowledge or think at all' (*LH* 90)), only, with her mother in mind, she keeps insisting that she will pull herself through. Indeed she keeps representing her mental crisis either as something her mother can prevent by giving her good advice or as something she has successfully overcome ('Am at last coming out of a "ghastly stretch of sterility"' (*LH* 306)).

Describing her daughter during the period for which there are no journal entries – namely, the time before and after her suicide attempt – Aurelia Schober Plath suggests that Sylvia Plath was 'absorbed for a while with each new personality she encountered and tried it on, later to discard it' (*LH* 134). Such protean ability to blend in and transform, so as to please one's addressee, can be seen as yet another version of the language of hysteria. Yet what Aurelia Schober seeks to highlight, given that she explicitly published these *Letters Home* as a response to the cruelly critical rendition her daughter offered of the same period in *The Bell Jar*, is that this hysterically protean Sivvy, who insisted on holding onto discords while she seemed to have forgotten childhood joys, who cynically searched ulterior motives beneath acts of kindness and love, was but a provisional version of the self, against which periodically her 'sunny optimism' would reassert itself. In so doing, however,

she supports conjectures that see all these voices as interchange-
able, even if some are more viable self-fashionings than others.
While *The Journals* are in part so compellingly irritating because
of the way Sylvia indulges in each new self-doubt with the same
excess with which she will then abandon it again, what
disconcerts the reader of these letters is the violent exclusions
of all deviancies upon which this return to optimism is based.
Sivvy initially fully accepts her mother's prohibition not to look
beneath the surface so as to privilege the marvellous moments
over the grimmer ones in her life. Indeed, along with recording
her academic, artistic, and amorous successes, she also repeatedly
designates the addressee of these accounts as a 'wonderful
mother'. It is as if – recalling the rhetoric of scepticism Sylvia
applies to her ideal mate in *The Journals* – Sivvy conceived of her
mother as perfect so that, as the daughter, who is quite literally
conceived in her mother's image, she must be perfect as well:

> You, alone, of all, have had crosses that would cause many a stronger
> woman to break under the never-ceasing load. You have borne
> daddy's long, hard death and taken on a man's portion in your
> work; you have fought your own ulcer attacks, kept us children
> sheltered, happy, rich with art and music lessons, camp and play;
> you have seen me through that black night when the only word I
> knew was No and when I thought I could never write or think
> again. (*LH* 240)

While in *The Journals* she practises a lack of distance between
herself and excessive melancholic anguish, abundant erotic
fantasies, and overwrought self-aggrandisement, the letters are
striking for the distance from emotional excess they exercise.
Janet Malcolm has noted that Sylvia Plath's duplicitous self-
presentation in these letters could be read as the sign not just of
a personal but also of a historical crisis. Recalling her own
experience of growing up in post-Second World War America,
she suggests reading these letters as a 'signature story of the
fearful, double-faced fifties'.[15] And yet, if one reads this
performance of duplicity – the excessive self-indulgence of the
journal entries and the equally excessive controlled buoyancy of
the letters – as the hysteric oscillation between various roles, at
issue is not whether one is more authentic than the other.
Rather, these letters obliquely address the traumatic knowledge
of a void at the navel of all self-constructions from which, as a

clandestine knowledge, they also shield the maternal addressee. The sense of horror haunts these letters precisely as that which is so unremittingly excluded from the image of untroubled self-confidence, flawless bliss, resilient strength to overcome all obstacles, as well as radiant trust in the future which she presents to her mother – be this in relation to her husband, her own work, or her public success. Equally disturbing is the sense that, rather than wilfully withholding information from her mother, Sivvy used these letters, addressed to her privileged representative of resilient survival, in order to make sense of the contingencies of her life. Precisely because she appears to have been under the obligation to relate everything to her mother, from acute depressions over rejections, egoistic joy at acceptances, the luck of her marriage and her maternity, to her psychic fatigue and physical ill health, one suspects she is inventing the happy narratives she imagines her mother wants to hear, so that, by virtue of this transformation into writing, she comes to believe in the strong, affirmative voice of the letters and uses it as a corrective against the anguished deliberations of her journal.

The duplicity inscribed in these letters, which stage how the hysteric cannot do without her master, even while she protests against this interpellative call, finds its most compelling articulation in the last letters Sivvy wrote to her Mother, when, under the strain of her marriage breaking apart, she no longer withholds the agonized side of her psychic life. Invoking this maternal representative of the law of survival, so as to reassure herself at a moment in her life when her fantasies of infidelity and abandonment had become hard reality, she exhibits yet a new voice – a sober rejection of all blind optimism coupled with self-confidence. As though she were progressively clearing away the layers of protective fictions with which she had endowed the portrait of her domestic bliss, she initially speaks only of a legal separation, to be kept quiet from everyone, and apologizes for her mother's ruined visit: 'I can never say how sorry I am you did not have the lovely reveling and rest I meant you to have' (LH 460). But about a month later, confiding her plans for divorce, she also prohibits any future visit from her mother: 'Also, as you can see, I haven't the strength to see you for some time. The horror of what you saw and what I saw you see last summer is between us and I cannot face you again until I have a new life; it would be too great a strain' (*LH* 465). Imagining her mother's disapproval of her fallibilities does not, however, lead to embarrassment and self-deprecation. Rather it is as though for the first time she were beginning to understand the maternal call for a golden mean, where accepting one's vulnerabilities need not cancel out a recognition of one's strengths. In the letter, dated 16 October 1962, describing her fever, she admits 'I need help very much just now', insists on sustaining a distance between her mother and herself ('Home is impossible. I can go nowhere with the children, and I am ill, and it would be psychologically the worst thing to see you now or to go home'), but also exhibits a buoyant self-certainty ('I am a genius of a writer; I have it in me. I am writing the best poems of my life; they will make my name' (*LH* 468)). Then, having reached the nadir of her sense of fallibility she again falls back on the voice of self-critical humour. 'Do ignore my last letters! I honestly must have been delirious', she writes on 18 October and continues by turning herself into a story: 'I guess my predicament is an astonishing one, a deserted wife knocked out by flu with two babies and a full-time job!' (*LH* 471).

Significant about this psychic shift, I want to argue, is the way it troubles any interpretation which seeks to privilege either the anguished or the self-confident voice as being authentic. If to the end she writes letters to her mother, accompanied by photographs, as though assuring both of them that in the midst of calamity all was well – 'I do hope these pictures convince you of the health and happiness of us three' (*LH* 491) – the point is not that Sivvy was projecting a false self, but rather that, responding to her mother's expectation of resiliency, she used their exchange to design a portrait of the young woman artist as survivor. Of course, read in hindsight, what also makes these letters so chilling is that we know how tragically the maternal call for buoyant stoicism failed. Insisting that she had to jettison the country in which her mother had set up their home entirely, when in her last letter to her mother she affirms, 'I have absolutely no desire ever to return to America. Not now, anyway' (*LH* 498), she seems to have lost this mitigating corrective to the scenario of scepticism performed throughout her *Journals*, in which, if she could not convince herself of wanting everything, she would find herself dangerously near to wanting nothing.

Commenting on this radical option between caring too much and not caring at all, Malcolm concludes, 'the journals and letters are the record of Plath's struggle against clinical and (if the two may be separated) existential depression by means of the various manic defences offered by the romantic imagination.'[16] Yet, what these journals and letters also chart is her cultivation of a distressingly ambivalent identification with symbolic laws as a psychic defence against her physical anguish as well as the mental distress. Negotiating her public identity in relation to social expectations readily transforms into a refiguration of her private relation to parental figures, such that her obsession with success, her desire to be recognized, her anxiety about being found wanting apply to both realms, just as the breach in trust in relation to her family members threatens to lead to a psychotic loss of world and suicide. However, while, in the course of deliberating on the question of gender and authorship, Plath quite explicitly recasts her situation as daughter such that it comes to stand metaphorically for her position within society, one wonders whether her desire to punish herself by invoking the harsh law of social ambition and failure, her desire to translate unsolvable contradictions into a situation of all or nothing, could not also be read in relation to her own cultural hybridity. Perhaps the dead father had not only come to haunt her as a symptom that something was lacking in her family. One could speculate further whether her deep need to be accepted, coupled with an equally deep fear about being found wanting, might not also draw on a sense of cultural displacement inherited from her parents, whose German–Austrian heritage made them foreign bodies in the New England of the Second World War. The Sylvia of *The Journals* does praise the more slow-paced European lifestyle over subjecting oneself to the 'commercial American super-ego' (*Jour.* 323), while the Sivvy of the letters will only agree with her mother's notion of America as a promised land with some qualifications – 'as long as we can stay out of the appalling competitive, commercial race, I'll be happy' (*LH* 287). Yet what is strangely left unspoken is any discussion of the way her preference for Europe, which she initially escapes to from the emotional impasse in which she found herself while a college student – 'Today a dream was planted: a name: England' (*Jour.* 57) – and then chooses as her place of exile, obliquely articulates her sense that, for her, America was from the start a provisional home. It is as though, in the process of immigration, her parents had disavowed their cultural identity, yet, as a secret which was to be kept, had passed onto their daughter the knowledge that, at the heart of their new home in America, was not just the loss of another home but also the suppression of both the father's German and the mother's Austrian–Jewish ancestry. In analogy to the way Sylvia Plath's romantic imagination and self-absorption served as a defence against the sense of a void at the heart of her existential being, one could surmise that the phantom of competition, for which her mother had become her privileged representative, could also be interpreted as a defence against the sense of a loss at the heart of her cultural assimilation. Her exaggerated need for success, her excessive desire to fit in, and her over-identification with the expectations of those from whom she wanted recognition not only exhibit her desperate urge to be certain of the recognition by others so as to convince herself of her own existence. Rather, they also exhibit her anxiety that, if she did not care excessively about belonging to a given cultural home, she would be forced to acknowledge her deeply ingrained sense of belonging nowhere.

3

The Poems

(O friend,
while the moon's bad,
and the king's gone,
and the queen's at her wit's end
the bar fly ought to sing!)

(Anne Sexton, 'Sylvia's Death')

In an interview she gave to Peter Orr in October 1962, Sylvia Plath explained, 'I think my poems immediately come out of the sensuous and emotional experiences I have.' Nevertheless she quickly qualified such a romantic bent by adding,

> I must say I cannot sympathize with these cries from the heart that are informed by nothing except a needle or a knife or whatever it is. I believe that one should be able to control and manipulate experiences, even the most terrifying, like madness, being tortured, this sort of experience, and one should be able to manipulate these experiences with an informed and an intelligent mind. I think that personal experience shouldn't be a kind of shut box and mirror-looking narcissistic experience. I believe it should be generally relevant, to such things as Hiroshima and Dachau, and so on.[1]

Although it is perhaps unclear in what sense a needle or a knife can inform cries from the heart, Plath's adamant rejection of an exclusively self-absorbed narcissism as the source of poetic expression highlights the importance she placed on control in the process of converting experience into poetry. As Mary Lynn Broe notes, even though the sheer vitality Plath celebrated in her poetry often takes no definitive shape, this linguistic expansiveness should not be read as an example for diffused emotions out of control, but rather as a consciously rendered love of motion and a self-conscious parody of existing prosody: 'Plath proves (by careful attention to her developing skills with sound,

62

rhythm, and imagery) that control – not the dictates of illness or indecision – governs her wide-ranging emotional exploration'. While a symmetry of verse and balance in poetic structure lead to the deployment of a fixed, changeless, even stillborn, energy in *The Colossus*, her later poetry, according to Broe, exhibits 'an ongoing, lively dialectic between inertia and energy in which the speaker continually takes different shapes, none final, all exploratory. Growth, motion, raucous humour, self-display and sleight-of-hand reversals all suggest a negative answer to her earlier question, "Is there no way out of the mind?" '[2]

Even though Plath's strict adherence to stanzaic and metrical structures as well as her skilful manipulations of prosodic predecessors support Broe's claim that we do her a disservice by reducing her œuvre to a summary of her themes, I want, nevertheless, to argue that it is precisely on the level of plot that one can locate her other most successful mode of controlling experience. As she translates the significant events of her psychic reality into fantasy scenarios about the origin and destiny of her desire, she does not only return steadfastly to a set of core themes. Rather, even while each scenario is continually refigured, the individual thematic complexes are also conceived as being interrelated, and thus in fact encourage a critical desire to construct an encompassing interpretative narrative. As Katha Pollitt notes,

> on the deeper level of themes and images, there was not so much a rift as a reformulation. Throughout her career, Plath worked with a tightly connected cluster of concerns – metamorphosis, rebirth, the self as threatened by death, the otherness of the natural world, fertility and sterility – and applied them all to what she saw as the central situation of her life, the death of her worshipped father when she was eight years old and the complex emotions of loss, guilt, and resentment it aroused in her even as an adult.[3]

If one of these recurrent scenarios involves the uncanniness of nature, which for Plath came so ambivalently to appear to be strangely enticing, solemnly serene, but also overwhelmingly threatening, these landscape scenes not only serve as a reflection of the perceiving subject, with the external scene giving voice to an internal emotion, but also stand in for an alterity that can never fully be subsumed under any aesthetic representation. Such an unresolvable ambivalence also applies

63

to Plath's other seminal fantasy scenario – namely, her refiguration of the family romance. Here, too, at issue is a confrontation with alterity, where an experience of the limits to an imaginative appropriation of another being recodes mis-recognition into images of violence. Finally a third recurrent scenario can be located in Plath's exploration of the oscillation between longing for extinction and transcendence of the self as this translates into fantasies of transformation, of escape from constriction and engulfment, and of flight, where casting off outgrown selves and overused masks leads to naked renewal. But, once again, the desire for a rebirth of the self brings into play the ambivalence explored in her other encounters with alterity, so that the paradigms nature, family, and self come mutually to stand in for each other. As Gilbert notes, finding herself enclosed 'in plaster, in a bell jar, a cellar or a wax house', the protean poetic persona emerging from Plath's poetry 'gets out by (1) killing daddy (who is, after all, indistinguishable from the house or shoe in which she has lived) and (2) flying away disguised'.[4] Yet the flight and the dramatically protean resurrection of the self are also terrible and the release from confinement is usually figured as a journey through death so that self-recreation and self-destruction are separated by a fine line. Accordingly, Blessing reads Plath's poems as the 'poetry of an escape artist' who incessantly seeks to release the energy of her psyche from its mortal wrappings, but points out that the protean forms she chooses privilege a scenario of horror: 'the vampire's daughter, the monster queen of bees, the victim of radiation poisoning, the Nazi artefact, the walking mummy with featureless face, the Medusa, the lamia, the paralytic, the zombie, the death camp victim, the Stepford wife.'[5]

Her thematic concern with discarding an old shape and practising the art of protean transformation, furthermore, also touches upon the question of prosody in that it is here duplicated by Plath's resilient ability to abandon an overused poetic style in favour of a new, invigorating one, once the early form was conceived as a confinement. Between the poems published in *The Colossus* and those published posthumously she had come to cast away her college training and the poetic formula she had learned as an English major, which had led her to cultivate a highly constructed and slightly archaic choice of vocabulary as well as an artistic form both endowed with erudite references to myths of antiquity and quite self-consciously calling upon the prosodically versed reader to note the terza rima, the rime royale, the couplets. As Ostriker suggests, 'the weakness of Plath's earliest work is that it is derivative and safe in style if not substance; and the strength of the poetry from 1960 on is achieved by means of a technique that has nothing to do with safety, everything to do with risk'.[6] Drawing a parallel between Plath's thematic concern with a flight from the identities inherited from her parents and her poetic liberation from formal confinement inherited from her reading and schooling, Ostriker speculates that 'having learned to see the skull beneath the skin, she threw away the skin'.[7] Yet Ostriker insists that this liberation should not be seen as a relinquishing of control and argues instead that 'this is free verse always approaching the older, stricter discipline, and gaining power from the tension' so that the rationale behind this free verse is to be seen as 'an attraction – repulsion toward formality.'[8] Indeed, in the same interview with Peter Orr, Plath explains that, adept at mimicking the tone of the great poets such as Auden, Yeats, and Dylan Thomas that had influenced her, what she found paralysing was not so much an anxiety of influence as a feeling of the full weight of English Literature on her, unsure whether she could measure up to these expectations.

Significantly the difference she herself came to locate between the poems published in *The Colossus* (which, she confessed to the interviewer, 'quite privately, bore me') and her new poems can be located in her abandoning the more traditional conception of the poem as a silent text, to be read in the absence of its author, to a notion of the poetic expression as a performance of vocal presence: 'I think that this in my own writing development is quite a new thing with me, and whatever lucidity they may have comes from the fact that I say them to myself, I say them aloud.'[9] Ironically, such an escape from the weight of English Literature was enhanced by leaving home to live in exile in the country of precisely this tradition, close to, yet also distinctly different from, the cultural home of her ancestors. As she explained to Peter Orr, though she considered herself to be an American in a general sense, she was also keenly aware of her German and Austrian background. Indeed, one has the sense that cultural dislocation came to offer her the platform for a balancing act between perpetual flight and the constraint of belonging and thus allowed her to develop her very particular poetic voice, inflected with inherited ties to European concerns (such as Dachau, Auschwitz, and Hitler's *Mein Kampf*), yet conceived in relation to the American poets (such as Robert Lowell, Anne Sexton, Theodore Roethke, and Elizabeth Bishop) she found so much more exciting than her English peers: 'I'm an old-fashioned American. That's probably one of the reasons why I'm in England now and why I'll always stay in England.'[10]

While still at Cambridge, Plath began to perfect her poetic refigurations of landscapes into scenes of psychic liminality. Some of these are tributes to 'the smashing nonchalance of nature', as in 'Channel Crossing' (*CP* 26–27), where, depicting a boat journey during a storm, Plath uses images of the onslaught of the sea's violent force to paint a scene of existential recognition. While other voyagers are stricken with seasickness, the poetic I, casting herself in the image of an angel, wrestling with casual blasts of ice, experiences this 'stark violence' as a moment of the sublime, because 'the mere chance | Of making harbour through this racketing flux | Taunts us to valor'. This experience of utter vulnerability, where 'stark violence lays all walls waste', however, has an exhilarating effect, for it allows the persona to 'strike a stance most mock-heroic', such that 'waking awe' at a 'rare rumpus which no man can control' merges with the reassuring gesture of concern, which, though realizing that this is perhaps nothing but a gesture of helplessness, she feels compelled to don. This sense of exhilaration experienced in the face of utter vulnerability is, however, intermediary. Having reached her destiny, she assumes her pose of normality again and, walking to shore over the plank with the other voyagers, she claims that no traces of this existential recognition will be carried back to the mainland: 'no debt | Survives arrival'. In other poems, like 'Winter Landscape, with Rooks' (*CP* 21–2), Plath paints a 'landscape of chagrin,' embellished with a black pond, a single swan, an austere sun heralding the beginning of dusk and ice-engraved reeds, whose bleakness works as a visual correspondence to her barren heart, waiting, like the landscape, for renewal: 'dry frost | glazes the window of my hurt.' Yet other nature scenes, such as 'Black Rook in Rainy Weather' (*CP* 56–7), address her longing that nature might serve as the scene for a moment of epiphany to descend upon her, clearly in imitation of the modernist poetics of Woolf and Joyce she had studied as an undergraduate. Watching a wet black rook 'arranging and rearranging its feathers in the rain', the lyrical I admits that it can expect neither a miracle nor an accident to render this random event into a significant portent. And yet, against the odds of probability, she holds onto the nostalgic recollection that

> a rook
> Ordering its black feathers can so shine
> As to seize my senses, haul
> My eyelids up, and grant
> A brief respite from fear
> Of total neutrality.

Locating the miracle that might allow her to 'Patch together a content | of sorts', for her psychic fatigue in such 'spasmodic | Tricks of radiance', the scene transforms into a celebration of liminality. In contrast to the two other poems discussed so far, this scene does not stage the recuperation from an experience of sublime transcendence or psychic barrenness. Rather the narrative's trajectory moves from nostalgic recollection, triggered by a random image, to a state of constant vigilance in anticipation of a moment of fully meaningful contingency:

> The wait's begun again,
> The long wait for the angel,
> For that rare, random descent.

Striking about all three of these early landscapes, however, is not only the conventionality of the images (the sea's unbridled force, the frozen heart, the portentous crow) but more crucially the manner in which they illustrate Plath's early use of poetic control, owing to which each poem stages a clearly demarcated scene, where the lyric persona, though fusing with nature, indeed discovering in the strangeness of the natural world an externalization of her private fantasies, nevertheless re-emerges as the agent of the event, even while the desires and anxieties expressed revolve around the experiences of self-expenditure and self-transcendence.

In what at the time she called her star piece, 'Mussel Hunter' (*CP* 95–7), Plath undertakes a different form of poetic control by quite self-consciously transforming a contingent event of nature into a formalized *danse macabre*. At dawn the lyrical I comes to the beach, looking for blue mussels to be used as free fish-bait. From the start the scene is permeated by signs of mutability ('mud stench, shell guts, gulls' leavings'), yet only as the lyrical I approaches the pool bed where the mussels hang does she begin to perceive the unrelentless alterity of nature. Though these mussels are conspicuous, she begins to sense 'a sly world's hinges had swung | Shut against me', causing her to imagine herself no longer as the self-confident agent of an intended action, but rather the object of nature's gaze. Owing to this shift from subject to object on the part of the lyric persona, nature's initial stillness begins to transform into a strange mobility, in the course of which the crabs not only animate natural phenomena, but in so doing endow it with a phantasmagoric quality:

> Grass put forth claws;
> Small mud knobs, nudged from under,
> Displaced their domes as tiny
> Knights might doff their casques.

These anthropomorphized creatures, slowly edging their way towards the pool mouth, take on the role of agent, while the lyrical I stands as if dumbstruck, trying to appropriate the strangeness of the scene by translating it into known categories. And yet precisely the question whether the crabs share the sensation of feeling mud between their claws as she would between her toes, ends any notion of communication:

> I
> Stood shut out, for once, for all,
> Puzzling the passage of their
> Absolutely alien
> Order.

As both go their way – the crabs into the pool and she to gather mussels – the poetic persona undertakes a second attempt at empathizing with the position of alien nature by imagining what she must look like to them. Yet, as if to underline the futility of this attempt, she suddenly finds an intact dead fiddler-crab whose carcass alone allows for the poetic appropriation she seeks. In contrast to the slipperiness with which the other crabs eluded her desire to transform them into a meaningful scene of mutability, she has in this inanimate carcass an object that will reassure her agency by supporting her urge to refigure the contingencies of nature into a coherent poetic narrative. The dead crab is stylized into the solitary artist figure, whose dead body not only transforms into a work of art:

> it
> Had an Oriental look,
> A samurai death mask done
> On a tiger tooth, less for
> Art's sake than God's.

At the same time, this crab's death, isolated from its peers, is interpreted as the heroic artist's defiance of any mediocre existence. In contrast to the other crabs, for whom she fantasizes an unspectacular dance of death in the midst of the water – 'Losing themselves | Bit by bit to their friendly Element' – this solitary death signifies valiant individualism: 'this relic saved | Face, to face the bald-faced sun.' However, even though this transformation of a dead object into a meaningful narrative confirms the power of imagination on the part of the perceiving I over all other alien natural phenomena, ambivalence prevails, for, in so far as this grimacing skull is refigured as the poetic persona's counterpart, its burnt face presages her own demise.

Supporting her interest in depicting landscapes as portentous scenes, bespeaking of human mortality, several of the early poems portray the liminal moment when night turns into day. In 'The Ghost's Leave Taking' (*CP* 90–1) early morning is described as a 'chilly no-man's land', a 'no-color void', a 'kingdom of the fading apparition', a 'joint between two worlds and two entirely | Incompatible modes of time', when seemingly meaningful dreams transform into the banal paraphernalia of everyday reality. On this threshold between the other world 'we lose by merely waking up' on the one hand, and, on the other, the harsh resurfacing of 'our meat-and-potato thoughts', the objects in her room appear to be hieroglyphs, speaking in the language of the strange dreamscape which defies 'mundane vision' much as the natural world does. And, as in the scenes of uncanny nature, where the imaginatively refigured vision of rooks and crabs transforms random elements into a miraculous epiphany, not only does this departing 'ghost of our mother and father, ghost of us, | And ghost of our dreams' children' recall the fantasy world of nursery rhymes, but, in its function as the nocturnal version of the sheets, 'Which signify our origin and end', it is also the harbinger of the 'dreaming skull', warden of the grave to which all nocturnal fantasy life as well as all diurnal bodily existence ultimately returns. While some poems, such as 'Waking in Winter' (*CP* 151), describe the dreamer's psychic voyage through 'destruction, annihilation', others offer equally threatening scenarios of nocturnal walks, such as 'Hardcastle Crags' (*CP* 62–3), where a young woman briskly leaves her 'dream-peopled village' behind, and, having passed the dairy herds, sheep, and birds, sleeping in the meadows, suddenly perceives this landscape in all its repelling alterity. Absolutely outside the human gaze – 'Unaltered by eyes' – it seems to loom stonily above her, threatening to crush her under this difference, forcing her to turn back.

Returning to the scenario of a solitary individual, caught in the awesome alterity of the natural world in 'Wuthering Heights' (*CP* 167–8), a poem belonging to the period after *Colossus*, Plath depicts the threatening experience of nature's over-proximity, but, although this poem is as carefully crafted as the earlier texts, thematically and syntactically it stages a significant shift in tone, for it explicitly privileges an unremitting destability of the perceiving subject. Choosing once again the narratorial stance of the first person, Plath begins with a depiction of the horizons as tilted, disparate, and always unstable faggots, surrounding her as she steps forward. Her imagination empowers her with the fantasy that these faggot horizons, if set on fire, might not only warm her but, more importantly, endow the pale sky with a more solid colour, and in so doing cast light upon the scene, which would allow her to orient herself within this undefined expanse of nature. Yet the landscape in fact prohibits such a stability in position, for, far from preventing the 'distances they pin' to evaporate, the horizons actually enhance her sense of dislocation – 'they only dissolve and dissolve'. In such a phantasmagoric setting where boundaries uncannily blur, the poetic persona finds herself drawn more and more toward self-expenditure – the wind is perceived as 'trying | To funnel my heat away', the heather enticingly invites her 'To whiten my bones among them', but, most significantly, she begins to feel completely disembodied as the gazes of the sheep transform her from perceiving agent to object of another's perception:

> The black slots of their pupils take me in.
> It is like being mailed into space,
> A thin, silly message.

And while, as in the earlier landscape scenes, nature is anthropomorphized – the sheep appear to her 'in grand-motherly disguise' – all signs of human presence are effaced. A house is metonymically reduced to unhinged lintel and sill; the only trace of living people is represented as the echo of 'a few odd syllables', moaned by the air. In contrast to the other landscape scenes discussed so far, 'Wuthering Heights' thus marks an enhancement of the fatal identity between the poetic persona and a miraculously portentous nature scene, not only because the lyrical I, by claiming 'The sky leans on me, me, the one upright', in fact suggests that it has taken on the shape of the deserted house. More importantly, the scene offers no escape. Not only does the poetic persona remain arrested as the sky's only support, gazing at the house lights in the valleys – 'narrow and black as purses' – but the final metaphoric turn, which compares this only source of light to the gleam of 'small change', fulfils her sense of self-expenditure. Having seemingly fused her poetic persona with the landscape, Plath's fantasy transforms the metonymy for neighbours – the house lights – into a metaphor for a fully unspecified light. Given that small change can gleam only as a reflection of another light source, the poem leaves the position from which this last image is to be read undetermined. As Jacqueline Rose notes, poems like 'Wuthering Heights' stage the inescapable hold that nature's alien, hostile power has over Plath's lyrical persona as a violence of unfathomability itself. Unsettling a clearly distinguishable location of agency or causality, Plath seems to be 'introducing a fundamental reversibility of agency that confounds active and passive and then dramatizes, through that confounding, the question of who is agent, who is victim, who (or what) suffers and who (or what) kills?'[11] Particularly striking about a poem like 'Wuthering Heights', is, then, not only the way that getting too close to the fascinating world of nature threatens the identity, and with it the power, of the poetic persona, even while the implied narrator continues to control the experience. Rather, the final metaphor dislocates the lyrical I from the speaking I, allowing the one to produce a controlled representation of the self-expenditure of the other.

In another nocturnal scene, 'The Moon and the Yew Tree' (*CP* 172), included in *Ariel*, Plath abandons the narrative mode altogether in favour of poetic pictography. In a far more static tone than the earlier landscapes, she sketches a passage from psychic to actual landscape, in the course of which a seemingly omniscient poetic persona, functioning as the gaze which animates this nocturnal scene, is exchanged for an impenetrable impersonal moon. At the beginning of the poem the light of the mind, cold, planetary, and blue, gives shape to an imaginary scene with black trees, 'Fumy, spiritous mists' and grass demurely grieving at the feet of this lyrical I, which, owing to the way her creative powers are located at the very centre of this vision, designates herself as a divine personage – 'as if I were God'. Yet from the start the stability of this subjective position is undermined by a recognition of visual fallibility: 'I simply cannot see where there is to get to'. Its rival, the white moon, is personified – 'no door. It is a face in its own right' – not, however, to suggest the possibility of a dialogue between these two sources of light. Rendering it as a face rather than as a door, Plath once again emphasizes the unremitting alterity of natural phenomenon. Its quiet, complete despair can be registered but not deciphered, and yet it is this unreadability which elicits the poetic persona's assertion of place – 'I live here.' This sense of belonging', however, leads back not to the actual house mentioned in the first stanza, but rather to a tenuous home – namely, her recollection of the sound of church bells on Sunday which 'startle the sky' as they affirm the Resurrection. Against this cultural edifice Plath pits the second natural phenomenon of the poem, the yew tree, whose anthropomorphized gothic shape forces the persona's eyes to move upwards and 'find the moon' in the place where in the prior stanza she had placed the sound of the Sunday bells. Now no longer the self-empowered poet, casting light on a scene, but, like a child, led in her gaze by the yew tree, the poetic persona imagines the moon as her mother. However, she conceives her as a horrific inversion of Mother Mary, who, rather than tenderly bending over her child, unloosens 'small bats and owls' from under her blue garments. And yet, even while the poetic persona now presents herself in the position of the humbled grasses, waiting for tenderness from the moon, what continues to frame the scene is the colour blue, though it has significantly shifted from being the 'light of the mind' to the moon's garment – 'Clouds are flowering | Blue and mystical over the face of the stars' – at the same time as the interior of the church is also imbued with this colour, so that, in correspondence with the clouds, 'the saints will be all blue | Floating on their delicate feet above the cold pews'. At the same time Plath resists any harmonic final meaning by emphasizing that, although the moon is the animator of this final scene, with her light calling forth the seemingly significant correspondences, she actually 'sees nothing of this. She is bald and wild,' much as the yew tree, whose shape is what induces the poetic persona to lift her gaze to this impenetrable maternal figure in the first place, is itself a hieroglyph: 'And the message of the yew tree is blackness – blackness and silence.' As in many of the other late nocturnal poems by Plath, the message that the night broadcasts to the lyric persona is how, though located in the world, its imaginative powers are fragile, so that the identity dependent on such a vision can be readily disseminated, leaving a disembodied subject, at home only in the nostalgic recollection of sounds and images; in the desire for tender recognition but finding itself actually placed in a world that is blind to it.

In many of her late pictograms, Plath continues to describe the experience of frozen marvel at the wonder of nature which characterizes her early landscapes, and yet, because the poetic persona seems to represent an event rather than narrate a scene, the perceiving subject appears to be far more removed. In 'Poppies in October' (*CP* 240) she records her astonishment that 'these late mouths should cry open | In a forest of frost, in a dawn of cornflowers' by sketching their difference to more likely sights, such as morning sun clouds, or the heart of a woman in an ambulance. The miraculous quality of this event, however, is also underlined by the comparison with metaphors of mortality. The poppies are rendered as the gift to a sky 'igniting its carbon monoxides', as a gift to unidentified onlookers, whose eyes are 'dulled to a halt under bowlers'. In some of these late poems Plath highlights the ominous quality of nature, as in 'Crossing the Water' (*CP* 190), where, concerned with the correspondence between 'the spirit of blackness' in humans and in natural phenomena, she offers a portrait of the shadows of the black trees and the black water that shake cold worlds from the oars of two black people in a boat. These are accompanied by reflections of dark advice given by the water lilies, which Plath conceives as 'expressionless sirens', as 'astonished souls'. In other landscape pictographs, however, she commemorates instead the wondrous persistence of life. In 'Among the Narcissi' (*CP* 190–1), for example, Plath offers a snapshot-like moment of harmonic correspondence between an octogenarian called Percy, 'recuperating from something on the lung', and the little flocks of narcissi he walks among 'in his blue peajacket'. What binds them together is the manner in which both the man and the flowers subject themselves to a higher law, and, by thus accepting their vulnerability, exhibit dignity. This mutual bond – of which Plath asserts 'there is a formality' – is, however, more than merely an external correspondence found in the blue colour both wear. Rather, as two versions of earthly existence, bowing and standing up again in the face of mortality, they form a bond of sympathy. The fatal attack of breathlessness, leaving Percy 'quite blue', induces a shared fright in the narcissi, which 'look up like children, quickly and whitely'. Similarly, in the 'Pheasant' (*CP* 190–1), the lyric persona pleads with a hunter not to kill this rare and kingly bird, a paragon of a creature which 'is simply in its element'. In its quality of belonging unconditionally to the world it becomes a source of wonder to her, crossing rarity with a right to exist, but also indicating to her in a thoroughly unthreatening manner, the provisionality of her own earthly existence: 'It was sunning in the narcissi. | I trespass stupidly.' Then again, as in 'Winter Trees' (*CP* 257), the astonishing wonder of nature's enigmatic language is quite self-consciously refigured as a botanical drawing, where the wet dawn is compared to ink blotting out the trees with fog. The impenetrable alterity of this scene is, as in 'Wuthering Heights', presented as unfathomability itself, only here, rather than threatening to engulf the persona watching the scene, it is fully distanced from any contact. The lyrical eye immediately translates this experience into a mythopoetic icon for feminine knowledge of the divine. The unknowable trees are compared to Leda and to Mary, who bore the fruit of divine intercourse, while keeping the secret of this knowledge of otherworldliness to themselves. At the same time, even such quiet serenity and seeming fusion between nature and divinity are never free of a threat to the poetic persona perceiving the scene.

In one of her last poems, 'Sheep in Fog' (CP 262), Plath once more returns to the notion that any unmitigated proximity to nature can threaten to engulf the lyrical I fatally. The scene is clearly one of dissipation. Beginning with the first image, 'The hills step off into whiteness', the poetic persona notes that the moving objects are perceived only by the traces that remain after they are gone: 'The train leaves a line of breath,' a passing horse emits the sound of hooves clapping and dolorous bells. Most striking, however, is the way in which, in the midst of such quiet yet unremitting resolution, the persona, presented as the object of nature's gaze, is passively drawn into self-expenditure:

> the far
> Fields melt my heart.
> They threaten
> To let me through to a heaven.

And yet this fatal destiny no longer has any anthropomorphized representation. It is even less recuperable into mythic language as the bald and white moon above the yew tree. It is unremittingly 'Starless and fatherless, a dark water', nothing but sheer materiality, the horrific inversion of a pleasurable persistence of life, described in poems such as 'Pheasant' – a persistence of life which exists outside and beyond any poetic consciousness giving it form, which continues to be even when imagination fails or has consumed itself. At issue in these late pictographs is not just the fact that Plath destabilizes our ability to determine who is the agent and who is the object of viewing, but rather that, in so doing, she also radically puts into question whether there is an agent at all who would offer a point of identification between the figured scene, the poet controlling the sensuous experience, and the reader. What Plath thus achieves with such terrifying candour could be called a rhetoric

75

of aporia – the poetic expression of absolutely controlled contingency, where the only meaning that can be applied to these scenes of gradual dissipation is the unfathomability of an expenditure of the poetic self, and with it, its world leaving us, the readers, alone with the void.

Though concerned with an entirely different knot of themes, Plath's poetic refiguration of the family romance enacts a similar gradual destabilization of the position of the lyrical person.[12] As I have discussed in the previous chapters, while *The Journals* predominantly explore the position of the daughter as a young woman and *Letters Home* primarily revolve around the mother as privileged figure of survival, Plath's most poignant family poems involve her imaginary refiguration of the father, whose death leaves her with a plethora of memory traces including the one landscape which, though lost, signifies home to her. In her autobiographic sketch 'Ocean 1212-W' (*JP* 117–24) Plath recounts how the line of beach, dividing the shore from the Atlantic, which she had known as a child is in fact 'the clearest thing I own. I pick it up, exile that I am, like the purple 'lucky stones' I used to collect...and in one wash of memory the colors deepen and gleam, the early world draws breath.' This childhood seaside is so inextricably linked to the figure of the father, however, because his death was the reason her family moved inland: 'whereon those nine first years of my life sealed themselves off like a ship in a bottle – beautiful, inaccessible, obsolete, a fine, white flying myth.' Working with this reciprocal transfer of imagery, Plath repeatedly invokes the lost father as a metonymy for this lost scene of childhood bliss, with both standing in for the state of happiness whose value resides precisely in its irrecuperability. In the same piece, however, Plath also recounts how this fine line between land and sea had fascinated her precisely as the border between life and death: 'If it could court, it could also kill. When I was learning to creep, my mother set me down on the beach to see what I thought of it. I crawled straight for the coming wave and was just through the wall of green when she caught my heels'. In the poetic refigurations of the father figure scenarios, revolving around a desire for the plenitude promised by a family and a home, concomitantly also revolve around an equally satisfying desire for self-expenditure.

76

In 'On the Decline of Oracles' (*CP* 78) Plath describes the 'vaulted conch' her father used to keep by his books, a crypt of sorts, given that it has retained 'voices of that ambiguous sea'. While the books and the shell themselves are given away to others after his death, the paternal gift she retains are fantasies that these lost objects have implanted in her image repertoire: 'I keep the voices he | Set in my ear, and in my eye | The sight of those blue, unseen waves' – a visionary power for prophecy. At the same time, however, her own sense of alienation is negotiated over the body of the lost father, for given that, in the course of mourning, her eyes have grown dull, the vision he has endowed her with has become useless. More crucially, in such early fantasy scenarios as 'Full Fathom Five' (*CP* 92–3), the father is himself represented as an unfathomable and dangerous phantom figure, who, although surfacing only very seldom, comes out of the sea to visit her. His most striking attributes are his white hair and white beard, spreading around him in the water, and these radial sheaves transform into a knotted bundle in which 'The old myth of origins unimaginable' can survive. Yet, as such a phantom, objectifying a gap in his daughter's knowledge – namely, the point of her own unfathomable origin – he is also an obscure and fey creature, always threatening to die again. Although his reappearance as a phantasmagoric effect of aquatic radiance proves 'The muddy rumors | Of your burial' false, undoing the linearity of time by turning the past back into the present, he is, nevertheless, a liminal figure. Only his head surfaces above water while below his shoulders he is fully rooted 'among knuckles, shinbones, | Skulls'. Because she imagines him to be a representation not only of a lost object but also of unfathomability itself, he remains inscrutable, defying her questions, depleting her: 'I walk dry on your kingdom's border | Exiled to no good'. And, as is the case with the gift of prophetic vision he bestows upon her, his phantasmagoric reappearance, which draws her to the border between the living and the dead, appears to be useless if not in fact precarious, for at the site where he surfaces the 'thick air is murderous'. The poem thus ends with the ambivalent comment, 'I would breathe water' – signifying both a desire to invigorate once more with moisture her psychic barrenness but also her suicidal urge to join the paternal water figure. At the same time her apostrophe of the dead father also attests to the power of her own imagination, for, as Barbara Johnson notes, 'If apostrophe is the giving of voice, the throwing of voice, the giving of animation, then a poet using it is always in a sense saying to the addressee, "Be thou mine." But this implies that a poet has animation to give.'[13] Indeed, Plath's refiguration of the family romance does not only serve to undo the temporality of paternal demise and thus restore her fantasy of an intact father–daughter bond. Rather her *mise-en-scène* of desire also transforms the daughter into the maternal figure, rhetorically giving birth again to the father, and in so doing overcoming her dependence on him as daughter as well as their shared dependence on mortality.

Although Sylvia Plath rejected the poem 'Electra on Azalea Path' (*CP* 116–17) for the collection *Colossus*, considering it 'Too forced and rhetorical' (*CP* 289), it is nevertheless interesting within the context of her poetic refiguration of the family. The scenario begins with the poetic persona, who, finding herself at her father's headstone, recalls her twenty-year imitation of his death: 'The day you died I went into the dirt, | Into the lightless hibernaculum'. Owing to this psychic liminality – this wintering – her imaginary powers allowed her to undo the tragic event, to repress his death and her guilt, which is to say she was able to sustain her fantasy of an intact family by placing a figure of divinity into the gap left by her father. Effacing his existence, she fantasizes an alternative family scene that transcends mortality: 'As if you had never existed, as if I came | God-fathered into the world from my mother's belly'. This is, however, not the only protective fiction she conceives to cover up the traumatic knowledge of death she has translated into a secret she shares with her mother. Finding herself in this uncanny liminality of recuperated innocence from death, indeed artificially detached from the facticity of the world, Plath also conceives her father as the protagonist of an eternal epic, in which 'Nobody died or withered on that stage'. Yet against this representation of the father, preserved against mutability in her psychic apparatus as in a crypt, Plath pits the reality of the grave and the carcass it harbours; his bones covered by six feet of yellow gravel, the specked stone marking his grave, the artificial red sage, whose colour the rain dissolves. This encounter with the cruel facts of death's irreversibility, however, does not force the daughter to wake up from her protective fantasies. Rather it induces a new fantasy scenario where her birth is conceived as a harbinger of his death: 'The truth is, one late October, at my birth-cry | A scorpion stung its head, an ill-starred thing; | My mother dreamed you face down in the sea'. Against her mother's mundane explanation that her father had died of a gangrene eating at his bone, she pits her interpretation whereby his death is seen as an act of punishing her for bringing her love to bear. This transformation of a contingent event into an epic narrative does not only recast the accident of his death into a story of destiny fulfilled. Rather, at stake in this fantasy scenario is the wish that, having woken from her twenty-year-long imitation of his death, she might again return to this uncanny position between life and death and share his crypt with him. Suddenly she is the phantom: 'I am the ghost of an infamous suicide, | My own glue razor rusting in my throat.' As a result of this transformation, her own fatedness and her empathetic identification with the dead paternal figure turn into mirror-images of each other, with her desire for her father and her desire for self-destruction appearing to be inextricably linked: 'It was my love that did us both to death'. It is, however, crucial to note that this guilt-ridden certainty that she is responsible for her father's demise, sharing his secret knowledge of death, in fact simply stages another version of the earlier fantasy scenario where, mimicking his death, the daughter was able to imagine herself and her father in a realm outside the transience of mortal existence. And as in the other father poems, apostrophe not only animates the addressed dead figure but endows the speaker with the creative power to give life to her own progenitor. Plath replays this fantasy of incest in 'The Beekeeper's Daughter' (CP 118), where Otto Plath, who had written a book called Bumblebees and their Ways, is once again resurrected from the dead and cast as a hieratical, 'maestro of the bees', moving among the hives in a priest-like but also enigmatically omnipotent manner. In this particular scene, the daughter, however, takes on various positions in relation to the desired object. While initially she fully subjects herself to him, indeed deanimates herself ('My heart under your foot, sister of a stone'), the second stroph gives voice to her identification with the queen bee and her fatal supremacy over all other bees: 'A fruit

that's death to taste: dark flesh, dark parings.' Finally, destabiliz-
ing all fixed locations, the last strophe represents her inside the
hive, kneeling down, setting her eye to a 'hole-mouth', so that in
this strangely encased position she can be penetrated by the
disconsolate paternal eye. This visual encounter significantly
stands as a trope not for a primal scene of her creation but rather
for a clandestine scene of paternal enjoyment:

> Father, bridegroom, in this Easter egg
> Under the coronal of sugar roses
> The queen bee marries the winter of your year.

In 'The Colossus' (*CP* 129–30) Plath returns to her fantasy of
re-creating the dead father, only here her idolization of his
absent body is presented as a colossal sculpture which she
inhabits. A fragmented body which she can never 'put together
entirely', the paternal colossus is at the same time an uncanny
figure, for from his dismembered mouth are emitted unfathom-
able yet portentous animal sounds, as though he were
reanimated by some unidentified outside force: 'an ora-
cle, | Mouthpiece of the dead, or of some god or other'.
Indeed, as Jean-Pierre Vernant argues, the Greek colossus,
standing in for the absent corpse, was meant to be a double of
the deceased, not a just image but an uncanny figuration
bespeaking an ambiguous presence which is also a sign of
absence. Rendered in stone, the deceased reveals himself at the
same time as he does so by speaking in the language of the
beyond.[14] In Plath's version of this Greek practice of substitution, dredging the silt from the colossus' throat so as to facilitate
her understanding of the words he speaks from beyond the
grave, mending the skull-places and the white tumuli of his eyes
so as to undo the scars of mourning, Plath's persona finds herself
fully fusing with this human-shaped ruin. At night she is
protected from the wind by squatting in his ear, at dawn she
watches the sun rise under his tongue. This shattered figure
signifies how her reminiscences allow her only an imperfect
configuration of the lost paternal body, with fantasy, however,
compensating this fallibility by virtue of exaggerating the
individual body parts into inhuman proportions. At the same
time, although her incessant mourning produces not just a
fragmentary but also an inanimate representation of the father,

this stony frame also proves to be a viable shelter from the contingencies of worldy existence. Drawn into its magical sphere, she finds herself turning from the living to the dead. No longer minding signs of other living beings ('the scrape of a keel | On the blank stones of the landing'), she seems to merge with the ruin she cannot mend: 'My hours are married to shadow.' Although, strictly speaking, Plath never gives voice to her dead father, these scenarios, staging her fusion with his dead shape, recall the rhetorical figure of prosopopoeia, which, as de Man has so persuasively argued, is inhabited by a latent threat 'namely that by making the death speak, the symmetrical structure of the trope implies, by the same token, that the living are struck dumb, frozen in their own death'.[15] This colossus prefigures not only her own mortality but also her actual entry into the petrified world of the dead, and yet, as in the other father poems, the gesture of self-extinction is inextricably enmeshed with that of poetic creation. The colossal stony figure she enters into as though it were a womb-tomb is a poetic rendition of the psychic representation of the absent father she has incorporated in the course of mourning. As such it is a figure of her own making, so that in these fantasy scenarios revolving around apostrophizing the dead father or responding to his call, refiguration of the dead, self-annihilation, and self-fashioning mutually reverberate.

The poetic refigurations of the father that were included in *Ariel* perform a radical shift in reminiscence. In 'Little Fugue' (*CP* 187–9) the black yew tree, starkly contrasted with the white featurelessness of a cloud, transforms into the eye of a blind pianist and then the keyboard at which he plays Beethoven's music – 'The yew hedge of the Grosse Fugue'. Against this harmony of big noises which she envies, produced by a blind man who can hear, she pits another Germanic voice, namely her father's, only his voice calls for obedient ignorance. In the course of this apostrophe his voice is transformed into

> A yew hedge of orders,
> Gothic and barbarous, pure German.
> Dead men cry from it.
> I am guilty of nothing.'

So as to undo the power of this paternal call for remaining blind, dumb, and deaf to the violence he represents, an interpellation she had covered up with idolizations in the previous mythic-inspired refigurations of her father, yet which she had at the same time preserved as a shared family secret, Plath renders this other German voice as a visual image: 'I see your voice | Black and leafy, as in my childhood.' The string of reminiscences that follows – her father eating sausages during the First World War, his blue eye colour, his briefcase containing tangerines – become tropes for murderous instincts, and in the course of her recollection, meant as an antidote to the blinding cloud of ignorance, she aligns her silence after her father's death to the silence of the slaughtered animals he ate. In this case, however, reanimating her dead Prussian father does not only allow her to resurrect the suppressed obscene figure of paternal authority that her prior scenes of paternal plenitude had occulted, so as to cast herself in the role of the one to whom death has occurred while she knew nothing about the law of mortality as well as the one who has grown lame in the course of her memory work. Rather, it also serves to accentuate the fluid boundary between different time periods, for the silence and the clouds of destruction she connects to this dead paternal figure ('This was a man, then! | Death opened, like a black tree, blackly') spill over into her present. Though she is a survivor of his death, and though she has now learned to transform her childhood ignorance into fantasy narratives, she also notes the continuation of this traumatic knowledge: 'Now similar clouds | Are spreading their vacuous sheets', for, looking at her fingers and at her child, she realizes that the clouds, her trope for the preservation of ignorance, transform into her marriage dress.

A similarly invocation of the horrific father occurs in 'Daddy' (*CP* 222–4), of which Plath said in a reading prepared for BBC radio: 'Here is a poem spoken by a girl with an Electra complex. Her father died while she thought he was God. Her case is complicated by the fact that her father was also a Nazi and her mother very possibly part Jewish. In the daughter or in her imagination, the two strains marry and paralyse each other – she has to act out the awful little allegory once over before she is free of it' (*CP* 293).[16] With the father now no longer a protective colossus but rather a 'ghastly statue', a constraining 'black shoe' she has lived in for thirty years, the poetic persona celebrates her belated patricide: 'Daddy, I have had to kill you | You died before I had time.' Yet, even though this new figuration of the dead father is meant to put closure on the process of mourning, in the course of which she had sought to recover him by virtue of imaginatively refashioning him outside the confines of mortal time, the paternal figure continues to function as a phantom, objectifying a gap in her knowledge. As she shifts from describing the ocean as his spectral place of residence to trying to find out the concrete location of his birth, a new gap in knowledge emerges. In this new fantasy scenario, collective and private disaster now come to be enmeshed, given that both his premature death and the two world wars have obliterated any traces of his home town. Not knowing his roots evokes the suspicion that some forbidden knowledge had been at the core of her family even before the traumatic scene of his death occurred, and, in order to mend the gaps in the narrative of her heritage, which she now perceives to be as critical as the father's premature death, she constructs a new family romance. If, in the earlier poems, invoking the lost father allowed her to give a name to her sense that something was awry in her home by blaming his absence, she now locates her psychic unease in the cultural affiliation he represented and had passed on to her. The omnipotent, protective father transforms into his obscene inversion, the terrifyingly brute Nazi stereotype 'panzer-man, O You – | Not God but a swastika' and, as she continues to explore the scene of incest ('Every woman adores a Fascist, | The boot in the face'), she now imagines for herself a Jewish mother, so that, by virtue of an identification with the victim, she can deflect her own guilt about the German ancestry inscribed in her blood. While, in the earlier poems, the father's premature death is the reason she cannot speak to him directly, the cause now is his obscene German language – 'a barb wire snare', 'an engine | Chuffing me off like a Jew' – metonymy for a politics of annihilation. At the same time, although Plath's poetic persona transforms her earlier nostalgia for an intact family into a nightmare vision of miscegenation and paternal sadism, with the father cast as a 'devil', a 'man in black with a Meinkampf look', seeking to torture and destroy her, this gothic fantasy is in fact fully consistent with the mythic father portrayed in 'Full Fathom Five', for he, too, is seen as drawing her like a siren to his residence beyond the world of the living.

And equally consistent with the earlier rhetoric of apostrophe is the fact that, poetically animating the father that has haunted her since his death turns into a story of her survival in a double sense. On the one hand, she comes to recognize that, in the course of her hysterical suffering from nonabreacted reminiscences, the dead father she had been so unwilling to relinquish has served as a psychic vampire, drinking her blood, regardless of whether this is in the guise of the benign ocean god or the malign Nazi torturer. Yet, along the lines of vampire lore, putting an end to his revenant existence – 'there's a stake in your fat black heart' – does not only mean terminating his power to haunt her, and with it his ability to draw her towards the realm of death. Rather, the discovery that the fertilizing bee-keeper father is nothing but a screen for the obscene sadistic father also allows her to sever herself from paternity entirely, and so to relinquish all responsibility for this cultural heritage. As she declares 'Daddy, daddy, you bastard, I'm through', she embarks upon yet another family romance, the fantasy of the orphan, no longer suffering from the reminiscences of a lost seaside childhood and its parental representative but rather fully innocent of the traces of the past – indeed so self-reliant in this utter dislocation from any family root as not to need any paternal addressee at all.

Maurice Blanchot, meditating on the way speech reveals being in its non-existence, suggests that, in the act of poetic self-formulation, 'I separate myself from myself, I am no longer either my presence or my reality, but an objective, impersonal presence, the presence of my name, which goes beyond me and whose stone-like immobility performs exactly the same function for me as a tombstone weighing on the void'. The ambivalence at the heart of such a poetic project consists in the fact that, even while literature is what endures after the rhetorical death of the speaker, it also persists in searching for the existence which precedes its formulation – namely, the contingent reality poetic speech excludes as it transforms random emotional experience into manipulated, controlled narratives; it seeks the 'abyss, Lazarus in the tomb and not Lazarus brought back into the daylight, Lazarus lost and not Lazarus saved and brought back to life.'[17] Given, then, that literature begins with the end, Blanchot concludes 'if we are to speak, we must see death, we must see it behind us. When we speak, we are leaning on a tomb, and the void of that tomb is what makes language true, but at the same time void is reality and death becomes being.'[18] It is precisely this gesture of ricocheting back and forth between being and non-existence, presence and absence, locating herself in social reality and expending herself in a void, which sustains Plath's most compelling poems about the murky interface between death-driven anger and the violence of incessant self-creation.

Already in an early poem, 'Tale of a Tub' (*CP* 24–5), her persona complains

> each day demands we create our whole world over,
> disguising the constant horror in a coat
> of many-colored fictions; we mask our past
> in the green of eden, pretend future's shining fruit
> can sprout from the navel of this present waste.

At the same time, she is convinced that these protective fictions, owing to which the psyche, like Lazarus, is brought back from a state of formlessness, will again be undone when 'death | shatters the fabulous stars and makes us real'. However, because she perceives social reality exclusively as a 'cracked world', redolent with 'incessant gabble and hiss' (*CP* 36), and as such an imperfect protection from the violence of raw reality, she also conceives of the world exclusively as something her perceptions create against the backdrop of the void of the tomb from which this self emerges. This resurrection occurs not only in the sense that she can learn to don the guises expected of her but more crucially in the sense that she can convince herself that the existence of the world depends on her perception of it. As the solipsist explains, when she shuts her eyes, 'these dreaming houses all snuff out', when she chooses to blink, the 'puppet-people' around her die, and the lover, though vivid at her side, is nothing but a phantom of her absolute imaginative power: 'All your beauty, all your wit, is a gift, my dear, | From me' (*CP* 37–8). Furthermore, from the very beginning of her project to transform emotional experience into controlled poetic expression, Plath also recognized external phenomena as insignias of her own mortality, as in 'All the Dead Dears', where the skeletons of a woman, a mouse, and a shrew, found in the Archaeological Museum in Cambridge, counterbalance her solipsistic animation of the world by presaging her return to the non-existence she has risen from:

> This lady here's no kin
> Of mind, yet kin she is: she'll suck
> Blood and whistle my marrow clean
> To prove it.
>
> (CP 70)

Other poems, in turn, though tracing a psychic journey into the absolute negativity preceding and subtending language, focus on the process of re-emergence back into daylight. The seven-part sequence 'Poem for a Birthday' (CP 131), initially conceived as a deliberate Theodore Roethke pastiche, came to mark the significant turning point in the development of Plath's poetic voice. It unfolds a fantasy of returning to the psychic condition that existed prior to having received a social identity, a 'name', which, fully in line with the Lazarus scenario presented by Blanchot, means situating this presymbolic psychic condition, in which the individual is not separated from her immediate presence and reality, in a tomb-like site. The scenario of disintegration begins in a shed during the late autumn:

> the month of flowering's finished. The fruit's in,
> Eaten or rotten. I am all mouth.
> October's the month for storage.

At the onset this storage space is compared to 'a mummy's stomach' so as to emphasize not only the proximity between the maternal womb and the tomb, but also the enmeshment of dissolution and regeneration. In this site Plath's poetic persona finds not only that she has regressed to an exclusively oral existence ('I am all mouth'), but, furthermore, that she identifies with the abject objects, inanimate as well as rotting, which are preserved in this crypt-like site between life and death: 'I am at home here among the dead heads', 'My heart is a stopped geranium', 'I am a root, a stone, an owl pellet, | Without dreams of any sort.' It is indeed through an apostrophe of the maternal body that this journey into the realm of unstructured, disseminated materiality can begin, into a psychic site which Julia Kristeva has called the semiotic chora subtending all processes of symbolization.[19] Imagining herself not only shrunken in size but also inside another body – namely, as the

86

tongue in her mother's mouth – she invokes a reversal of birthgiving: 'Mother of otherness | Eat me.' Once inside the cavern of her own making, she takes on a variety of shapes – mother of other animals, navigator through marrowy tunnels, then again the offspring of a root, the bride of rubbish, keeping time 'among emmets and mullusks', a 'Duchess of Nothing'. As though to emphasize the complete lack of any hierarchical structure at work in this void of the tomb, remembering nothing at all, becoming another, asking for a new name is coterminous not just with the sense of being engulfed by alterity but with herself incorporating all the dead, rotten, and inhuman life around her: 'I must swallow it all.'

The phase of resurrection in turn sets in with an experience of indolence, forgetfulness, and drowsiness, heralding a state of non-existence that is 'not death', but 'something safer', but then moves on to a vivid phantasmagoria of witch-burning. As she rapidly transforms from being an inhabitant of her own wax image to the caged pet of a 'black-sharded lady', the lover of a 'hairy spirit', and finally a rice kernel, about to be consumed by 'the red tongues' enveloping her, she now moves from the experience of being disseminated among many shapes, connected with the void of the tomb, to an experience of a complete loss of shape, of absolute negativity, connected with the transformation through fire: 'I am lost, I am lost, in the robes of all this light.' Yet, falling out of this violent light, she finds herself first diminished to the shape of 'a small pebble', only to be mended, in an operation scene whose gothic tone recalls Frankenstein's fantasy of fashioning life from inanimate matter even while it refers back to her own reanimation of the dead father figure in 'The Colossus' – her eyes and ears are chiselled open, sponges mollify the 'flint lip', volts of electricity reanimate her, while catgut is used to stitch her fissures. Though her 'mendings itch', she reassures herself, 'I shall be good as new'. In that it ends with a fantasy of being re-created from dead matter, the entire sequence not only articulates a passage through psychic dissolution but also addresses precisely the interface between death and language that Blanchot locates at the heart of the Lazarus myth. What makes not only the mending so compelling but also the entire language within which this passage is described ring true is its reference to the materiality of a non-existence of the subject, the dislocating expenditure of the self in nothing.

Joyce Carol Oates has astutely diagnosed Plath as 'one of the last romantics', who 'acted out in her poetry and in her private life the deathliness of an old consciousness, the old corrupting hell of the Renaissance ideal and its "I"-ness, separate and distinct from all other fields of consciousness, which exist only to be conquered or to inflict pain upon the "I"'.[20] Such radical isolation of the ego, she suggests, results tragically in an inability to identify with anyone or anything, since the Other, be this nature or another human being, always threatens to overwhelm, engulf, victimize, and destroy the romantic subject. Furthermore, as Oates concludes, this 'dread of being possessed by the Other results in a failure to distinguish between real and illusory enemies', which is to say in a psychic impasse: 'if everything unusual or foreign is an evil, if everything new is an evil, then the individual is lost.' Indeed, as the discussion of Plath's landscape poems and her refiguration of the family romance has shown, rebirth often transforms into a scene of dissolution. Like a double image of one and the same hospital scene, two poems, both written on 18 March 1961, focus on the way that the reality of the void and the existence of death continue to inhabit one's being even after a psychic re-emergence from the tomb. In the first, 'In Plaster' (*CP* 158–9), Plath's poetic persona describes her division into two selves: 'This new absolutely white person and the old yellow one.' The perfection of the superior one ('She doesn't need food, she is one of the real saints') is, from the start, coupled to her death-like quality. Though unbreakable in 'her whiteness and beauty', a paragon of slave mentality with 'her tidiness and her calmness and her patience', helping the old body mend, never complaining, grateful to be the container for another's growing body, this perfect cast is also perceived to be 'like a dead body'. The relation between these two versions of the self turns into a battle between two aspects of death becoming being. To the superior white cast, seeking to cover up all fallibilities and imperfections, the old yellow self represents a 'half-corpse' whose hairy and ugly body with all its fallibilities and imperfections needs to be concealed under the mask of saintliness. The intense relation between them is such that, while the old self realizes she is so dependent on this external role of perfection that she has quite 'forgotten how to walk or sit' without her, she also realizes that her immaculately refashioned self functions like her own coffin, threatening to cover her up entirely, fully to encase her and take her place. Precisely because their coexistence cannot last peacefully, the poetic persona decides that, as in 'Daddy', where she had to kill the father figure once the shoe would no longer do, so, too, she must avenge herself by escaping from this encasement, allowing it to 'perish with emptiness'.

If we read this poem in conjunction with the other hospital scene, 'Tulips' (CP 161), we come to recognize that, even while the death-urge can be deployed to cast off a role of perfection which has come to signify a life of living death, its inversion is an embrace of the void as reality. Here the persona describes her slow transformation into a self-contained corpse-like being. Learning to blend in with the white peacefulness all around her in the hospital room, she has given up her social identity and her possessions – 'I am nobody' – and this sense of purification is coterminous with relinquishing all identity along with her emotional ties to the world. Having been swabbed clear of her 'loving associations' to the objects she used to possess (her teaset, her linens, her books), and which had endowed her with a series of social identities, she now no longer hangs onto her name nor her addressees: 'I am a nun now, I have never been so pure.' Yet, in contrast to the other poem, in this scenario the figure of vengeance is not only a force external to the self but, furthermore, a part of nature more alive than she. Watching the tulips, she does not only note that 'Their redness talks to my wound, it corresponds'. Rather, like sirens, their red tongues upset and oppress her by speaking to her of the self-expenditure she desires. Indeed, they have come to take the place of the domestic associations ('My husband and child smiling out of the family photo' she had relinquished), and in so doing they once more fill the gap of an interpellative call, in response to which her identity can take shape. Only now the pull is not towards the constrictive social role constructed with death behind but towards the reality of the void. Having experienced the serenity of complete dislocation, being nowhere, committing herself to nothing, bare of all associations, the persona finds herself relocated in the gaze she ascribes to the tulips:

I see myself, flat, ridiculous, a cut-paper shadow
Between the eye of the sun and the eyes of the tulips,
And I have no face, I have wanted to efface myself.
The vivid tulips eat my oxygen.

As Jacqueline Rose has pointed out, what is crucial about Plath's female figures of transcendence and self-immolation is not so much the question whether they harbour creative or destructive attributes. Instead what is poignant is that they illustrate how 'we do not in fact have a term for an identity free of the worst forms of social oppression which does not propel us beyond the bounds of identity in any recognisable form'.[21] Once Plath's romantic ego relinquishes constrictive social roles, it can know nothing other than the void itself. Thus her feminine figure of vengeful anger or death-aimed anguish incessantly performs the fluidity of the boundary between being and non-existence, with the subject either haunted by traces of the traumatic knowledge of the void subtending any symbolic identities or possessed by the equally traumatic recognition that all symbolic identities are lethal confinements so that the only way out of this impasse appears to consist in embracing fatality itself. In the fantasies she conceives so as to organize her relation to this traumatic knowledge of the presence of death in life, either she dissolves the casts that force her into social identities felt to be a living death, or she destroys the figures of authority in response to whom she feels compelled to assume these constrictive identities, or she immolates herself. Significantly the one scenario she does not find satisfactory involves simply accepting the enmeshment between poetic speech, social identities, and death's uncanny presence in the midst of human existence as a productive exchange, much as in her *Journals* she is unable to escape the sceptical impasse of wanting everything or nothing. In 'Elm' (*CP* 192–3) this vengeful figure of transcendence threatens to haunt her addressee with a 'voice of nothing', which harks back to a prior experience of madness, as well as with a voice of unquenchable dissatisfaction, which insists that 'Love is a shadow', precisely because she cannot fully shed the traumatic knowledge about the void of the tomb out of which her poetic language emerges. As though this clandestine knowledge were a revenant and she the host it has chosen to feed upon so that she in turn comes to spread this contagion of fatal knowledge, Plath's anguished persona explains:

> I am inhabited by a cry,
> Nightly it flaps out
> Looking, with its hooks, for something to love.
> I am terrified by this dark thing
> That sleeps in me.

In 'Apprehensions' (CP 195–6) Plath's persona, donning the role of a prophetic seer, conceives of herself as confined by a plethora of walls she is compelled to read for their portentous messages, all of which, however, ultimately bespeak her terror at the inescapability of mortality, even while she rhetorically calls out for a liberation from these fatal insignias: 'Is there no way out of the mind.'

In other poems, such as 'Birthday Present' (CP 206), death is presented as the yearned-for shedding of precisely these constrictive walls of the romantic ego, given that they force her to speak so uncannily with her back to an open grave: 'Only let down the veil, the veil, the veil', she calls out to the bearer of a mysterious gift: 'If it were death | I would admire the deep gravity of it, its timeless eyes.' Immediate death would be a noble birthday, for it would jettison off forever with one pure and clean cut the external world, whose air, though others perceive it as being clear, is for her already infested with lethal carbon monoxide. Then again, in 'Fever 103°' (CP 231–2), Plath's figure of transcendence equates her body heat with an act of purification, shedding her sin and her love from her like scarves. The dangerous radiation she emits does not only wreak vengeance on others, 'choking the aged and the meek', killing the 'weak | Hothouse baby in its crib', and as though to threaten her husband, 'greasing the bodies of adulterers | Like Hiroshima ash and eating in. | The sin'. Rather, as her internal heat and her self-sufficient light turn her into an instrument of destruction, she also assumes divine proportions. Explaining to her beloved, 'I am too pure for you or anyone. | Your body | Hurts me as the world hurts God', she fantasizes her imitation of Maria's ascension:

> I think I may rise –
> The beads of hot metal fly, and I, love, I
> Am a pure acetylene
> Virgin.

As she sheds all lovers, she can also dissolve all the protective and supporting selves to whom they were addressed, for in her state of utter purification these identities appear to be nothing more than 'old whore petticoats'. Similarly in 'Ariel' (CP 239), riding her horse transforms into a fantasy scene where flight is coterminous with an unconditional embrace of self-expenditure. Unpeeling all constrictive social identities ('Dead hands, dead stringencies'), she relinquishes not only her symbolic name but with it the distance between herself and any unmitigated reality, transforming herself into pure energy:

> I
> Am the arrow,
> The dew that flies
> Suicidal, at one with the drive
> Into the red
> Eye, the cauldron of morning.

In other poems, as in 'Purdah' (CP 242–3), the vengeful figure of transcendence, waiting for her bridegroom to arrive so that in his presence she can unleash the lioness from inside the protective cast ('the small jeweled | Doll he guards like a heart'), directs her anger primarily at others. Or, speaking explicitly as a feminine Lazarus (CP 245–6), Plath's resurrected figure of vengeance compares her suicide's body first to that of the victims of the Holocaust ('my skin | Bright as a Nazi lampshade', 'My face a featureless, fine | Jew linen'), then to a 'big strip tease', a 'theatrical | Comeback in broad day', which attracts a great audience because she is such an adept performer at this miracle: 'Dying | Is an art, like everything else. | I do it exceptionally well.' And yet at issue is not just Plath's insistence that her poetic language allows her to transform the reality of the void and the being of death, which Lazarus experienced in the tomb, into a controlled form that in turn will enable an audience to partake of this experience in such a way that by proxy this experience of a dissolution of the self 'feels real' to them. Rather she also insists that partaking of this knowledge has a price: 'there is a charge.' Even while the onlooker, cast in the figure of the doctor as torturer, seems to have control over the disempowered woman, he runs the risk of being himself infected by this voyeuristic touch of death. As Lady Lazurus, Plath's vengeful figure of transcendence is both victim and agent. She recasts her sense of the stifling fatality of social identities into a metaphor of the Holocaust corpse – 'So, so Herr Doktor,' she mocks, 'I am your opus, | I am your valuable, | The pure gold baby | That melts to a shriek.' As this imagined enemy pokes and stirs these remains of living substance, these traces where 'there is nothing there', he is, however, himself drawn into an exchange with her equally killing energy that has been liberated from these constrictive shells:

> Beware
> Out of the ash
> I rise with my red hair
> And I eat men like air.

In a letter written on 21 October 1962 in response to her mother's demand that she write about decent, courageous people, Plath counters:

> Don't talk to me about the world needing cheerful stuff! What the person out of Belsen – physical or psychological – wants is nobody saying the birdies still go tweet-tweet, but the full knowledge that somebody else has been there and knows the worst, just what it is like. It is much more help for me, for example, to know that people are divorced and go through hell, than to hear about happy marriages. Let the *Ladies' Home Journal* blither about those. (*LH* 473)

Accordingly in 'Mary's Song' (*CP* 257), written roughly a month later, she directly relates her own psychic anguish, her sense of being haunted by violence, anger, and a death wish, quite explicitly to the traces of violence left over from the Second World War in the European homeland of her parents. Because she perceives that the ousted Jews, emptied into the heavens, 'float/Over the cicatrix of Poland, burnt-out | Germany. | They do not die', she can only conceive of the social reality within which she is asked to locate her identity as a death-infested and death-threatened site:

> a heart,
> This holocaust I walk in,
> A golden child the world will kill and eat.

At issue in all these figurations of the female figure of vengeance, transcendence, and self-immolation, however, is the fact that, even while they perform the hysteric's ability to fit in and constantly change shape, to embrace new roles with utmost passion only to relinquish them effortlessly in favour of new ones, this protean shift in identity revolves very definitely around a kernel – namely, the knowledge of the void as reality. In other words, at stake is not that Plath's poetic persona lacks identity, but rather that she is so rigidly constructed in relation to two fatally entwined interpellative calls. On the one hand, Plath explores the way social reality calls forth white plaster-cast protective fictions of the self but also figurations of the *femme fatal* as lioness, radiation agent, or red-haired phoenix. On the other hand, she explores the way the reality of death, calling forth an ecstatic enjoyment of self-expenditure, can be liberating when she is refigured as an empowered agent of motion and energy, flying through the air like an arrow or ascending to paradise as a purified virgin. But death's call is also staged as a debilitating experience – namely, in those poems where a response to death is refigured as a scene of entering the maternal womb-tomb where, utterly disempowered, she is reduced to the passive material upon which its powers of dissolution work. She appears similarly victimized in those poems where death emerges as an articulation of the inevitability of transgenerational haunting, refigured as the scene of the European holocaust, in which, defenceless, she is exposed to paternal violation. As I have already argued in relation to the self-fashionings explored in *The Journals* and *Letters Home*, one does Plath a disservice by seeking to reduce the trajectory of her poetic negotiation of the burden of gender, cultural tradition, and family heritage into an issue of whether these figures of transcendence are false or authentic, veiled or naked, deceptions or real. Rather, even the most radical of these figurations should still be seen as an expression of poetic control, of her ability to contain the traumatic experience of life's exchange with death, as well as an expression of her fear that, if a crisis in imagination were to occur, there would be nothing to set against the empty grave she so urgently felt to lie behind all her poetic figurations. In one of the poems she wrote so frantically in the early mornings of the winter of 1963, while her children were still asleep, 'Totem' (*CP* 264), Plath knots these two points of reference together. Commenting on the resilience of social identities, she claims:

There is no terminus, only suitcases
Out of which the same self unfolds like a suit
Bald and shiny, with pockets of wishes,
Notions and tickets, short circuits and folding mirrors.

And yet, even while the energy of such protean self-creation is seemingly inexhaustible, she also insists all human activity is 'Roped in at the end by the one | Death with its many sticks'.

In one of these last poems, 'Child' (*CP* 265), she does explore another, less death-infested theme, namely, her maternity – so as to pit the life-sustaining interpellative call of her child ('Your clear eye is the one absolutely beautiful thing') against her bouts of psychic anguish and anger (the 'troublous | Wringing of hands, this dark | Ceiling without a star'). And yet, while the products of natural procreation attest the power of survival, the creation of perfect aesthetic forms proves to be itself a source of death, for 'perfection is terrible, it cannot have children' (*CP* 262). In what is perhaps her most astonishing poem, 'Edge' (*CP* 224), Plath came to draw together all the many sticks death uses to make its beat heard in a poetic language which both shields from and feeds upon its knowledge. Invoking the antique myth of Medea, Plath portrays a maternal figure of death, holding her two dead children at her breasts. This stark image is above all so shocking, however, because, in contrast to the other scenes of feminine immolation, all violent energy, all anger and anguish, have been transformed into a far more horrific gesture of utter acceptance of fatality:

The woman is perfected.
Her dead
Body wears the smile of accomplishment.

As in some of her very late landscape scenes, Plath here performs a rhetorical aporia, for, although her rhythm and imagery are highly controlled, the scene she depicts is one where the power of language seems to have utterly dissolved. As she describes the terrible perfection of the dead body, leaving the reader undecided whether this is yet another version of herself as figure of fatal transcendence, or whether she is in the position of the survivor, Plath emphasizes that any attempt at transforming this contingency into a narrative about destiny is a protective fiction on the part of the spectator from which the truth of this event inevitably recedes; it is the 'illusion of a Greek necessity', which 'Flows in the scrolls of her toga', just as 'her bare | Feet' merely 'seem to be saying: We have come so far, it is over.' The other witness to the scene, the moon, 'staring from her hood of bone', is also no longer a source for interpretation. Instead, indifferent because 'She is used to this sort of thing', she speaks in an unfathomable and unrelated voice, 'Her blacks crackle and drag'. This pictogram of feminine death, uncannily written one week before Plath's actual demise, stages what Slavoj Zizek designates as a symbolic suicide, the act of losing all, of withdrawing from symbolic reality, of renouncing renunciation itself. In such a fantasy scenario, after the protagonist has passed 'through the "zero point" of symbolic suicide', and begins anew from the point of absolute freedom, of abstract negativity, he explains, 'what a moment ago appeared as the whirlpool of rage sweeping away all determinate existence changes miraculously into supreme bliss',[22] and in so doing leads to the awareness that we have nothing to lose in loss. What Plath achieves in this last poem could be called the crisis of imagination perfected, when there is nothing more to say about death's incursion, because all strife-driven energy and tension have been spent, and when all resistance against the threat of engulfment by alterity has been relinquished, because poetic expression and the emotion of self-expenditure it is meant to control have simply amalgamated.

In a short piece, 'Context', commissioned by the London Magazine in 1962, Plath commented on the relation between her poetry and any political context in the following manner: 'My poems do not turn out to be about Hiroshima, but about a child forming itself finger by finger in the dark. They are not about the terrors of mass extinction, but about the bleakness of the moon over a yew tree in a neighbouring graveyard. Not about the testaments of tortured Algerians, but about the night thoughts of a tired surgeon. In a sense these poems are deflections. I do not think they are an escape' (JP 92). Indeed, coming to these poems after the event of her death as well as the myth about her poetry of confession, which has taken hold of our collective image repertoire in its wake, one feels compelled to add that, perhaps, it is not just that they are not an escape. Rather they persistently proclaim the fact that escape – be it from the confinement of social roles, the restrictions of cultural laws, the burden of one's family heritage, the obsessions of one's psychic reality, or finally the urge towards death – though constantly refigurable in poetic expression, is ultimately impossible.

4

The Prose Writings

> The title women and fiction might mean, and you may have meant
> it to mean, women and what they are like; or it might mean women
> and the fiction that they write; or it might mean women and the
> fiction that is written about them; or it might mean that somehow
> all three are inextricably mixed together and you want me to
> consider them in that light.
>
> (Virginia Woolf, *A Room of One's Own*)

Released one year before Sylvia Plath entered Smith College,
Stanley Dolan's musical *On the Town* tells the story of three
sailors who, enjoying a twenty-four hours' leave in New York
City, encounter three representatives of the Post-Second World
War American woman – a taxi driver, who continues to do a
man's job even though the war is over because she will not give
up what she enjoys, an anthropologist who indulges in fantasies
about the sexual potency of the prehistoric man, and finally the
protagonist, Ivy Smith, a girl who has come to the city from a
small middle American town so as to become a musical celebrity
only to find herself earning her money as a belly dancer in a
booth on Coney Island. While the other two women are
resiliently self-assertive, unabashedly giving voice to their
desires and getting what they want, and in fact far more
confident and streetwise than the sailors, the figure of Ivy Smith
serves to illustrate how the notion of perfect womanhood,
which took hold in the wake of the Second World War, required
a complex strategy of duplicity. To keep up the front that she is a
success in New York, Ivy finds it necessary to lie to her parents
about her dubious source of income and, having been chosen to
be the 'Miss Turnstyles of the Month', she convincingly poses
for photographers in the guise of a self-assured and happy
urban celebrity. Indeed, to underline how the all-round

accomplished American girl could be nothing but a fiction, Stanley Dolan in fact introduces his heroine by virtue of a fantasy sequence, in which the protagonist and co-director Gene Kelly, seeing her beaming face on a poster, imagines the qualifications of this New York glamour girl (played by Vera-Ellen) who can apparently do everything. In this dance number, she is initially shown as a home-loving girl, cheerfully ironing, and, when her husband comes home, immediately bringing him a newspaper and a pipe, and yet within seconds she transforms into a public star. She exhibits high-society elegance as she suavely glides among deep red satin curtains, demonstrates patriotism as she proudly marches with officers of the army and the navy, but then again, in the guise of a frail and flower-like creature, she is shown to have exquisite aesthetic taste, dancing and painting at symphonic hall. The longest part of this fantasy sequence, however, is dedicated to illustrating her athletic abilities. Sprinting and running she is shown to come in first, proudly waving the trophy over her head. As a football player, she successfully catches the ball and runs with it, and finally, boxing against a bevy of strong white men, she beats all her adversaries. As the scene ends with her sitting triumphantly on a pile of eight knocked-out men, the fantasizer exclaims, 'Gee, what a girl.' In the course of the film, however, Gene Kelly discovers not only that Ivy comes from the same town as he but, more importantly, that she is only too willing to exchange her assumed celebrity as well as her artistic aspirations for precisely the fiction of domestic bliss his fantasy began with, before abandoning it for more flashy scenes of public fame. Though, fully in line with the ideology of the time, we are asked to believe this to be Ivy's authentic self, the film's irony feeds off the fact that throughout we have actually been shown that suburban domesticity is but one of many pretences women have learned to cultivate so as to please the stronger sex.

Written with precisely this highly contradictory image of accomplished femininity in mind – the composite woman who is not only a subservient homemaker, but also professionally ambitious, sexually rapacious, indeed physically stronger than men but above all successful, happy, and self-confident in whichever role she takes on – Sylvia Plath's most compelling prose explores the toxic side effect of this cultural construction.

As in *The Journals*, she uses her prose to deconstruct the myth of American assimilation, which had taught her that, 'After all, we could be anybody. If we worked. If we studied hard enough. Our accents, our money, our parents didn't matter' (*JP* 35). In these texts, the very first of which were written with the readers of commercial women's magazines such as *Seventeen* and *Mademoiselle* in mind, Plath sought to bring back to light all the ambivalent emotions that had to be covered up, denied, or repressed in order for the fiction of successful self-fashioning to hold – the radical lack of understanding between the sexes inherent to the very notion of the heterosexual bourgeois couple, the madness lurking beneath professional ambition and accomplishment, as well as the fact that, in the midst of any effort at refashioning oneself beyond one's ethnic, class, and family heritage, the legacy of one's biological parents inevitably returns to haunt. Janet Malcolm has suggested that there was something fundamentally duplicitous about the American culture Plath's acerbic prose depicts with such a canny sense for something being amiss. Recalling that the world in which both Sylvia Plath and she came of age was one where the need to keep up pretences was particularly prevalent, with all those who had survived in a post-Hiroshima and post-Auschwitz world desperate to believe that these catastrophes had left American society unchanged, Malcolm confesses, 'we lied to our parents and we lied to each other and we lied to ourselves, so addicted to deception had we become. We were an uneasy, shifty-eyed generation. Only a few of us could see how it was with us.'[1] While Plath did not come directly to confront the horrors of the death camps and the atomic bomb until her late *Ariel* poems, from the start many of her stories set out to analyse the implications of this culturally sanctioned rhetoric of deception – the lies we tell ourselves to make sense of the world and convince ourselves that we fit in, the lies we live to assure ourselves of being loved and acknowledged, but also the tragic cost of such pretence.

However, although many of her stories as well as her novel *The Bell Jar* are pitted against a generation of parents desperate not to speak, regardless of whether they were perpetrators, victims, or liberators during the Second World War, and ruthlessly enmesh private anguish with political disaster, what is particularly striking about Plath's prose is that, in contrast to the iconoclastic style of her late poetry, it voices her discontent within fully conventional narrative style of precisely the mass culture she sought to critique. As Jacqueline Rose notes, critics have tended to ignore not only the way Plath's desire to be published in magazines such as the *Ladies' Home Journal* was one of her most persistent concerns, but also that she was perfectly happy to revise her prose so as to satisfy a very specific set of formulas and demands.[2] Writing to her mother on 14 March 1953, she explains, 'I'll never get anywhere if I just write one or two stories and never revise them or *streamline them for a particular market*. I want to hit *The New Yorker* in poetry and the *Ladies' Home Journal* in stories, and so I must study the magazines the way I did *Seventeen*' (*LH* 107). The ambivalent contradiction her narratives thus perform is that, on the one hand, she seeks to broadcast a message about the collective resonance to private stories about romantic jealousy and abuse, social misrecognition, and public persecution, in the course of which the intactness of American suburbia is disclosed as screening out encrypted shared secrets. On the other hand, in line with the ambivalence of feeling so characteristic of the language of hysteria, she fully believed in the values and laws of the very culture whose authority she also sought to dismantle. Precisely because her desire to disclose the traumatic knowledge subtending the American myth of plenitude and infallibility went hand in hand with her ambition to become a successful and publicly recognized author, she came to realize that she could not tell her stories outside her culture's discursive formations but rather had to enact an ambivalent contradiction – the non-coincidence between her traumatic sense of personal dislocation as well as her sense of uncanniness at the heart of the home and her aspiration to produce texts that would fit the expectations of the market. In so doing she came to perfect what Judith Butler has called performativity, a 'reiterative and citational practice by which discourse produces the effects it names', such that 'the force of the regulatory law can be turned against itself to spawn rearticulations that call into question the hegemonic force of that very regulatory law.'[3] The cultural performativity Plath exhibits in her prose writings is such that it offers narratives which trouble any easy identification with the image of the happy, healthy, successful American family, but do so in the very terms of the culture they seek to interrogate. Skilfully deploying the rhetoric of gothic humour and scathing parody allows her to exaggerate and thus put into question the regulatory law, to point to what exceeds it, what is excluded from its domain even while never breaking with its narrative codes.

As Linda Wagner notes, one of the pervasive concerns of the stories published in the posthumous collection of Plath's prose writings, *Johnny Panic and the Bible of Dreams*, is that of 'individual difference and a culture's fear of what it sees to be the unusual'.[4] In several stories dealing with the gender of creativity, she presents scenarios in which her female protagonist can define her sense of self only in rivalry to her masculine mate's artistic work. In 'Day of Success' (*JP* 185–98) Ellen, wife to a struggling young author, Jacob, finds her domestic peace suddenly threatened by a phone call announcing that her husband's play has been accepted by a major London producer. Comparing herself to her friend Nancy Regan, whose husband had already achieved celebrity as a playwright, but in the process had abandoned his wife for an actress because the former 'simply couldn't compete – in looks, money, talent, oh, in anything that counted' (*JP* 188), Ellen begins to fantasize a scene of desertion. Her jealousy of her husband's sudden success not only augments her awareness of her own lack of imagination and artistic skill but, given that the entire scenario is played through with the jilted friend Nancy in mind, also serves to highlight her sense of not being an accomplished wife. Feeling herself critically assessed by the editor of a prestigious magazine, who has dropped in unexpectedly to pick up a copy of the play, she convinces herself of her own failure ('Already I don't fit. I'm homespun, obsolete as last year's hemline'), and going through fashion magazines only confirms her awareness of 'the gulf separating her from the self-possessed fur, feather and jewel bedecked models who gazed back at her from the pages with astoundingly large limpid eyes' (*JP* 191). As though imitating the scene of jealousy so lavishly described at the end of the second part of the *Journal*, Plath develops the producer's secretary, Denise, into a phantom figure, whose function it is to objectify her heroine's sense of a lack at the heart of her domestic bliss. Though she knows only her voice from the ominous phone call, Ellen's conviction that she will end up deserted like Nancy, nourished by this friend's gossip about the martini-drinking redhead being 'a legend, one of those professional home-wreckers', turns this imaginary rival into the insignia of her own failure. As she waits for her husband to return, she oscillates between dressing up as a vamp and indulging in her role of motherhood only to find out, upon Jacob's return, that all her fears were unnecessary. Destroying her hallucinations of betrayal with one fell swoop, he announces that he has used the royalty cheque to make a down payment on the country cottage they have been longing to buy. And yet, although Ellen seems to have recuperated her sense of domestic safety, smugly telling her friend Nancy that, as a country wife, she will no longer need her help as fashion consultant, the sudden force with which her rivalry erupted allows Plath to articulate the violence which needs to be contained for the precarious and duplicitous fiction of the happy artist couple to hold.

Far more direct in its dismantling of the conventional gender of creation, however, is her representation of the vindictive jealousy a wife feels for her husband's seemingly superior imaginative powers in the 'Wishing Box' (JP 48–55). Each morning at the breakfast table, the protagonist, Agnes Higgins, finds herself caught in a hopeless battle with her husband, Harold, for, while she is unable to recall her dreams, the vivid nocturnal fantasies he recounts 'over his morning of orange juice and scrambled eggs', constructed as 'meticulous works of art', certify that he possesses 'an astonishingly quick, colourful imagination'. Although Agnes's manifest explanation for her infuriation over Harold's 'peculiar habit of accepting his dreams as if they were really an integral part of his waking experience', has to do with her sense of being left out of this 'life among celebrities and fabulous legendary creatures in an exhilarating world', an exile from a large part of her husband's psychic reality, Plath discloses a fatal strategy of duplicity in her heroine's psychic reality. The problem with Agnes's nocturnal fantasy world is precisely not that it is empty, but rather that it is horrifically filled with 'dark, glowering landscapes peopled with ominous unrecognizable figures', which she desperately seeks to repress upon waking up, even while she withholds these 'fragmentary scenes of horror' from her husband. While she interprets her reticence as a sense of feeling inferior in her own powers of imagination to the 'royal baroque splendour' of her husband's fantasy world, what Plath suggests is that, in lying about her nocturnal fantasies, Agnes seeks to cover up the cracks that have begun to show on the surface of her domestic life. Far from being less creative than he, she is in fact astutely responding to the vacuity of her situation with amnesia or scenes of horror. Not only is she an exile in her own home, because, as the narrator of the story explains, her husband is in fact indifferent to her fantasy life given that 'his own dream-life preoccupied him so much that he'd honestly never thought of playing listener and investigating his wife's dreams'. Rather, she is also an exile in the sense that Sigmund Freud argues we are never master in our own house because our unconscious speaks to us about the fallibility, anxiety, and psychic discontent that can never fully be severed from any fiction of the self as happy, perfected, and fully appeased in its desire.

Put another way, what Plath discloses is that Harold's ability to escape into a perfectly constructed world of fantasy is coterminous with a form of self-absorption that not only requires a blindness towards all fragmentary and imperfect scenes of psychic horror, but also results in a fatal indifference towards the world outside his imagination. Agnes's response to her sense of dislocation is first a nostalgic reminiscence of the 'fertile childhood days', when, imitating the fairy-tale stories she was reading, she would produce 'benevolent painted dream worlds', including a vivid 'dream about Superman, all in technicolor'. And because she has accepted the dictum of her culture that only positive and perfectly intact fantasies of the self attest to creativity, these imitation fairy-tale dreams implicitly stand for a lost happiness she believes she could regain, were she to retrieve her shaping imaginative powers. Once her husband tells her to 'practise imagining different things', in the manner he has taught her, she frantically seeks to exchange her imaginary life (the fragmentary scenes of horror she wishes to keep hidden) with the culturally sanctioned fantasies of an immaculate existence, for she has bought into his claim that her inability to produce the dreams he expects of her is a sign of a 'gaping void in her own head'. Foraging through all the products of mass culture she can find – novels, women's magazines, newspapers, cook books, shopping catalogues, travel brochures, films, and finally TV – she tries to master her husband's art of exchanging both the 'utterly self-sufficient, unchanging reality' of the outside world as well as any sense of psychic anguish into artificial dreams of plenitude, success, and recognition. The cruel irony with which Plath ends her parable about the terrible psychic cost of adjusting to a world of duplicitous happiness is that, in seeking to efface the voice which recasts her domestic life into fragmentary scenes of horror, by exchanging it with simulacra fantasies nourished not by past experiences or the reality around her but rather by the fictions of popular culture, Agnes actually comes to perform with her whole body the void in her own head she has sought to ward off. Addicted to alcohol and TV, she is now able to transform reality into fantasy, but at the same time finds her mind condemned 'to perfect vacancy, without a single image of its own', and, with the capsules her physician has given her for her insomnia, she tragically rearticulates her husband's dictum that she translate her discontent into perfect fantasy scenarios. The corpse he finds, 'dressed in her favourite princess-style emerald taffeta evening gown, pale and lovely as a blown lily, eyes shut, an empty pillbox and an overturned water tumbler on the rug at her side', functions as a materialized sign, embodying and disclosing in one and the same gesture, the death inscribed in his belief in living in self-constructed fictions. With the last image of Agnes's secret smile of triumph, signifying that she is 'at last, waltzing with the dark, red-caped prince of her early dreams', Plath's story offers a double comment on the fatality of a belief in duplicity. Not only does Agnes's suicide illustrate that the only way to ward off the horrific truth underlying fantasies of plenitude and intactness is a dolled-up corpse. As a symptom of her husband's imaginative powers, it also signifies the murderous undertones of Harold's indifference. For the self-absorbed daydreamer, privileging his own fantasy world over their shared domestic reality, she had always been nothing other than a doll. And yet, particularly disconcerting about this last image is that, owing to the references to popular culture as the source for Agnes's fatal materialization of foreign fantasies at her own body, we cannot overlook the social implications of such an exclusive preoccupation with fictions of the self. It is in such images that Plath's prose offers a reiteration of the regulatory law of bourgeois marriage because it allows her narrative to exceed the very codes it also deploys and in so doing succeeds in disclosing that the American wife who fully lives the cultural texts presented to her is nothing other than a dressed-up dead body – dead to both her childhood fantasies of plenitude and her adult nightmares about the fallibilities that go hand in hand with human existence.

In 'Johnny Panic and the Bible of Dreams' (*JP* 17–33) Plath offers yet another version of how an inability to control one's dream work can lead to psychic alienation. The protagonist, working as an assistant to the secretary in the Adult Psychiatric Clinic, finds herself becoming addicted to the dreams she is asked to type up. A psychotic fantasy scenario unfolds, in which she imagines the world as a battlefield between Johnny Panic, the author behind all dreamwork, and the director of the clinic, 'studying to win Johnny Panic's converts from him by hook, crook, and talk'. The protagonist undermines her allegiance to the restorative effort of the doctors and instead sees herself as secretary to Johnny Panic himself. Her work at the clinic comes to serve her personal education as 'dream connoisseur. Not a dream-stopper, a dream-explainer, an exploiter of dreams for the crass practical ends of health and happiness, but an unsordid collector of dreams for themselves alone. A lover of dreams for Johnny Panic's sake, the Maker of them all.' She soon discovers that her 'real calling' does not consist in simply typing up dreams but rather memorizing them so as to reduplicate them at home. At the same time she becomes adept in identifying people who come into the clinic by their dreams, teaching herself to uproot unspoken dreams from mere chance remarks and thus re-creating dreams that have not yet been spoken. Once transcribing and collecting current dream data no longer satisfies her, she plots to explore all the old record books, believing some of the best dreamers to be found there. As in the other stories, Plath depicts her protagonist so fully exiled in her alternative fantasy world that she has become oblivious to her actual surrounding. The heroine decides to spend the night at the clinic so as to be able to submerge herself into the forbidden records without the threat of being discovered, and in fact

106

concocts plans for spending all future weekends there as well, as though seeking to exchange this vicarious feeding off other people's fantasies for the vacuity of her own psychic reality. In contrast to 'The Wishing-Box,' however, we are not given an outside perspective on the process of delusion that has taken hold of the narrator. Instead, the scene in which she finds herself caught by the director of the clinic the next morning is rendered as a gothic scene of inquisition and torture, related from her distorted perspective. Fancying Johnny Panic's top priests in the room with her, she clings to the old notebook so as to assure them of her allegiance to their mutual master, while the director of the clinic and the secretary of the Observation Ward overpower her. Ending with a grotesque description of electrotherapy, where the protagonist perceives the doctors as 'false priest in white surgical gowns and masks whose one life work is to unseat Johnny Panic from his own throne', the story ultimately leaves open whether the violence about to be inflicted on her body is the beginning of healing or the final step into the realm of panic. As the heroine enters into the void beyond all fantasy, thinking she has become lost to the figure of obscene paternal authority which has given meaning to her existence, albeit the conviction that all psychic work reduces to an addiction to externally induced fantasies, the 'face of Johnny Panic appears in a nimbus of arc lights on the ceiling overhead'. Once again the reiteration of the regulatory law Plath offers in this narrative takes on the form of a psychic impasse, with the protagonist locked between the scylla of a duplicitous life of happiness and health and the charybdis of nightmare and madness.

In other prose texts Sylvia Plath came to be more direct in her critical interrogation of a culture that sought so forcibly to tailor the 'rebel, the artist, the odd' into an 'Okay Image', such as the description of her initiation into a college sorority in 'America, America' (JP 34–8), where, at the end of one week of abuse by a Big Sister, she comes to the decision 'Somehow it didn't take – this initiation into the nihil of belonging. Maybe I was just too weird to begin with'. Similarly in another, more lengthy fictional account of social rituals of debasement, 'Initiation' (JP 137–47), she describes her heroine Millicent's sense of triumph at deciding not to join the sorority after all the efforts on the part of her initiator to destroy her ego so she would fit in with the sought-after social norm. Other stories more directly involve her sense of being an exile in the suburban America of the early war years, owing to her German heritage. In 'Superman and Paula Brown's New Snowsuit' (JP 160–6) the first-person narrator, a fifth-grade girl living opposite Logan Airport and fascinated with the freedom of flight this place of take-off and landing comes to represent for her, articulates her nebulous sense of not fitting into her Winthrop world by dreaming of flying. These 'nightly adventures in space began', she explains, 'when Superman started invading my dreams and teaching me how to fly'. Not only is this nocturnal fantasy a reworking of her daily reality, for her Uncle Frank, who lives with her and her mother because her own father is dead, seems to bear 'an extraordinary resemblance to Superman incognito'. Rather, along with her friend David, who shares her love 'for the sheer poetry of flight,' she relives the radio programme she hears each night before supper the next day during recess, with both using this game to place themselves apart from the other children. So as to underscore the adolescent ignorance at work in her protagonist's re-creation of these fantasies of flight, Plath introduces the boy Sheldon Fein, who comes to stand in for the villain in her heroine's Superman games, during which he becomes a Nazi, borrowing the 'goose-step from the movies', even while the narrator briefly mentions the fact that his uncle is actually a prisoner in Germany. Equally oblique is the narrator's mention of her Uncle Frank saying 'something about Germans in America being put in prison' for the duration of the war.

These war games, inspired by a radio programme, are suddenly effaced by two actual events, in the course of which the heroine again re-creates the scenes presented to her as a media event in reality. Meant as a special treat, all the children attending her friend Paula's birthday party are taken to the cinema, but preceding the main feature, *Snow White*, they are shown a war movie about Japanese prisoners. That night, the heroine finds herself unable to conjure up Superman so as to block out the horrifying images of prison-camp life she has seen. The story comes to turn on the ironic fact that, once more translating her nocturnal fantasies into a daytime game, the heroine finds herself in the position of the American prisoners. During a game of tag, another boy pushes Paula, who falls into the mud and spoils her snowsuit, yet the other children turn her into the scapegoat. She perceives them as facing her 'with a strange joy flickering in the back of their eyes', as they claim 'You did it, you pushed her', until she is not only utterly confused as to what really happened, but is now quite concretely in the position of the outsider she had played during her Superman games. What Plath, of course, is working with is the girl's ignorance of the fact that, in the fantasies of her neighbours, she is a representative of the German aggressor – a threatening foreign body present among them which must be labelled as different and ostracized. This point is made, though once more obliquely, in her mother's overwillingness to buy Paula a new snowsuit, so as to avert any possible further repercussions, over and against her daughter's insistence that she is innocent.

Ultimately the story is perhaps too overt in naming its theme – the loss of innocence in the face of an onslaught of real political strife: 'Nothing held, nothing was left. The silver airplanes and the blue capes all dissolved and vanished, wiped away like the crude drawings of a child in colored chalk from the colossal blackboard of the dark'. It is, nevertheless, interesting in light of the fact that Plath returns to explore her own ambivalence of feeling in relation to her German father in another story, 'The Shadow' (JP 330–9), written four years later. In one of the entries in her Smith journal she had noted, 'My present theme seems to be the awareness of a complicated guilt system whereby Germans in a Jewish and Catholic community are made to feel, in scapegoat fashion, the pain, psychically, the Jews are made to feel in Germany by the Germans without religion. The child can't understand the wider framework. How does her father come into this? How is she guilty for her father's deportation to a detention camp?'[5] As in the earlier story, Plath once again chooses to articulate her paranoia of being culturally other by virtue of a scenario where a child, accused of having committed a crime – in this case biting her playmate Leroy Kelly in the leg – is unable to vindicate herself. In both stories, the incursion of political reality into her childhood fantasy world, as Jacqueline Rose notes, 'signifies the simultaneous collapse of her comic heroes', and her own, moral world'.[6] And yet, there is a significant shift in the narratorial presentation of this fantasy scenario, for, in contrast to the earlier story, not only is the father still alive, but rather he is also the parent who supports her in her decision not to apologize 'in spite of the neighbourhood pressure', at the same time that he quite concretely turns into the victim of political prejudice against German-Americans. While the earlier story follows the chronology of the events, relating first the scene of the children's game and then the heroine's denial of guilt, the second story significantly begins with the protagonist's reading of the event: 'By rights, I should have been let off easy with a clear verdict of self-defence, yet this time, for some reason, the old Washington Street ideals of fairness and chivalry didn't seem to count.'

As in the earlier story the heroine bonds in her games with the neighbourhood boy over their mutual admiration for radio shows such as *The Shadow*, and *Lights Out*, and does so, furthermore, precisely because she does not want to be identified with his doll-playing sister Maureen. But, in contrast to the earlier story, this childhood crime is more complex. Using what she has learned to be one of the powerful ruses of femininity, the sister, not getting the scissors she wants, calls to her brother to help her and then, translating the situation into a comic book scene, pulls the rug from under the heroine's feet, as he had seen the Green Hornet do to a spy. In this position, with Leroy sitting on her stomach and Maureen, squatting beside her and tickling her, the heroine finds she can liberate herself only by biting her adversary in the leg. In other words, in this story she is actually guilty of the crime she is accused of, and, far more explicitly, at stake is the transgression performed both by her gender crossing as well as by the way all three children are implicated in the violence that results. Furthermore, the turning point of the story is not that she cannot vindicate herself because her mother seeks to forestall any further repercussions of the war-inspired prejudice against German-Americans, but rather the uncanny spilling-over of the children's misunderstanding into political reality. In the course of the next months the heroine discovers that not only she but also her parents are slighted by the neighbours long after she and Leroy have become friends again. As in the earlier story, she also watches a film about Japanese war prisoners, and, once again, the morality she has learned from her consumption of comic books and radio programmes is shaken: 'my sure sense of eventual justice deserted me.' As in the earlier story, the breakdown of her fantasy that, although there is evil in the world, the powers of good would always protect her involves the spilling-over of these fantasies into reality, only here Plath is far more concerned with the way everyone in the neighbourhood is implicated in the children's game of reading the world as though it were a comic-book battle between spies and the powers of good. One day Maureen tells the heroine, 'My mother says it's not your fault for biting Leroy,' only to add, she 'says it's because your father's German'. In a sense the neighbourhood replays the scene in the Kellys' living room, only now her father is in the position of the spy, and pulling the rug from under his feet translates into his deportation to a detention camp for German citizens.

The ironic turn in this second story thus consists in the heroine's exculpation. While in the earlier story she is forced to take on the responsibility for something she did not do, in the latter she is relieved of her responsibility because her action is no longer judged as an individual event. Rather, reduced to the stereotype – 'daughter of a German' – she cannot personally be held accountable for a bestiality that is considered to be part of her essence, being a trait inherited from her father. While she is thus exonerated from a crime she did commit, her father is punished for crimes that he is completely innocent of. In the course of this transformation, her personal fantasy of being an outsider, which, owing to her mass-media consumption, she casts in 'such elementary colors', is uncannily mirrored by her neighbours' paranoia, which also refuses to allow for any grey zones. The other ironic aspect of this text, written three years before the poem 'Daddy', is that it uncannily foreshadows her own fantasy about the paternal figure of authority as a prototypical Nazi. Although in 'The Shadow' Plath stages her victim scenario by representing an identification with first-generation German-Americans, she already sketches the perpetrator scenario she will explore in the later poem – namely, in the oblique comments the other children make about the father's cultural guilt. Crucial is that, in both the fictional and the poetic rendition, the narrator does not only find herself in the position of victim, be it of the prejudices of her peers or of her own conjectures about paternal violence. Rather, both fantasy scenarios also aim at clearing her of any traces of the guilt connected with her German parentage, be it because the protagonist's father is punished in her stead or because the poetic persona has constructed for herself a family romance where the mother is explicitly Jewish.

The Bell Jar, Plath's autobiographical novel about her time as a guest editor at *Mademoiselle Magazine* in New York, her nervous breakdown and suicide attempt that summer, and her reconvalescence, for which there are significantly few entries in *The Journals*, was published under the pseudonym Victoria Lucas in London by Heinemann, in 1963, one month before her suicide.[7] To her mother she had written on 25 October of the previous year, 'Forget about the novel and tell no one of it. It's a pot-boiler and just practice' (*LH* 477). In a letter Patty Goodall wrote to Mrs William Norton, a friend of Aurelia Schober Plath, immediately after her visit to Plath on 19 January of the same year, she confirms that Sylvia 'seems to recently have had some success in publishing a book. Whether this is intended to be passed on, I don't know, but will leave it up to you whether to tell Mrs. Plath. Perhaps she knows. Sylvia seemed shy about the subject, saying it was being published under an assumed name – I didn't question her further' (*LH* 497). Thus duplicity was written into the production of this novel from the start, for even while Plath offers a scathing critique of the bustle of the New York publishing world and the sanctimonious smugness of suburban life, she not only does so in the thoroughly popular style of the potboiler, but also seeks to keep up the pretence of being the conscientious American daughter in exile by publishing under an assumed name. Furthermore, as Jacqueline Rose has pointed out, although the pseudonym was nominally assumed to have been meant to protect individuals who might recognize themselves in the story, 'it has a more obvious meaning here in relation to cultural difference, for the pseudonym is one of the hallmarks of popular fiction'. Taking Plath's claim seriously that her novel was a mere potboiler, Rose suggests that

> From the unnamed women's magazine where she is guest editor, to *Ladies' Day*, *The New Yorker*, *The Christian Science Monitor*, the scandal sheets, cinema (technicolor football romances, *Gone with the Wind*,

the Bette Davis movie made out of her benefactress's book), and, in passing, the *Reader's Digest*, *Vogue*, and *Life* and *Time* magazines – it is the range and density of cultural reference in *The Bell Jar* that is so striking.

In so far as this novel can be read as the 'autobiography of the coming-into-being of a writer across the fragments of contemporary cultural life', most striking about these peregrinations through disparate strata of high and low art, Rose concludes, is that 'Far more than the male literary tradition, it is popular writing, and especially popular writing by women, which oppresses – and generates – the woman writer in *The Bell Jar*.'[8]

In the following discussion of *The Bell Jar*, I want, therefore, to concentrate on two aspects of Plath's representation of the toxic side effects of the post-war American myth of happy, healthy, and successful good living. First, the regulative law of this culture, connected to the various mother figures in the novel, ranging from her own mother, to the mother of her fiancé, her benefactress, the editor of the fashion magazine, and finally her therapist, is shown to be the catalyst for her suicidal madness but also the interpellative call for recuperation and survival. Secondly, Plath's move into popular fiction brings with it a shift in tone from the highly self-conscious prosody of the early poems and the violence and rage of the *Ariel* poems, to a narrative voice marked by self-irony, able to describe the pathos of cultural dislocation, the horror of a self-consuming madness, even while at the same time stepping away from this overflow of destructive feeling. By virtue of humour Plath comes to perfect the cultural performativity she had experimented with in her earlier prose writing, with parody emerging as the narrative strategy that allows her to dismantle the very discursive formations whose regulative law she also finds herself unable to abandon fully, by simultaneously celebrating the artificiality of fantasies of health and happiness and pointing to the horror beneath the perfect surface. Indeed, when she reflects upon her suicide attempt in *The Journal*, she records her own psychic ambivalence about how to narrate this event, admitting both her debt to the serious plot of Virginia Woolf's modernist aesthetics, as well as her inbuilt proclivity towards the plot resolution of women's popular culture:

I was getting worried about becoming too happily stodgily practical: instead of studying Locke, for instance, or writing – I go make an apple pie, or study *The Joy of Cooking*, reading it like a rare novel. Whoa, I said to myself. You will escape into domesticity & stifle yourself by falling headfirst into a bowl of cookie batter. And just now I pick up the blessed diary of Virginia Woolf…I feel my life linked to her, somehow. I love her – from reading *Mrs. Dalloway*…*To the Lighthouse*. But her suicide, I felt I was reduplicating in that black summer of 1953. Only I couldn't drown. I suppose I'll always be overvulnerable, slightly paranoid. But I'm also so damn healthy & resilient. And apple-pie happy. Only I've got to write. I feel sick this week of having written nothing lately. (*Jour.* 152)

If, then, we follow Jacqueline Rose's cue and read Plath's novelistic rendition of this fateful summer as a potboiler, yet another aspect of the duplicity inherent to her mode of narration comes to the fore. As Ted Hughes notes, one of the contradictions written into the structure of *The Bell Jar* consists in the fact that, even while the plot celebrates a belief in sublimation and rebirth, it never fully sheds the traumatic knowledge that the protagonist Esther Greenwood's anguish cannot be healed because traces of clandestine madness will always haunt her. In the final pages of the novel, the heroine walks into her interview with the board of doctors, confident that she is healthy enough to be released, and yet she notes, 'How did I know that someday – at college, in Europe, somewhere, anywhere – the bell jar, with its stifling distortions, wouldn't descend again' (*BJ* 254). Reading *The Bell Jar* as staging a battle between two disparate novels, Hughes argues, 'While she tries to impose her protective, positive interpretation and nurse the germ of an authentic rebirth, in her nativity ritual, the material is doing something quite different… [the symbolism] discloses a pattern of tragedy like a magnetic field in the very ground of her being', and in so doing troubles the belief in making good things happen by affixing this recuperative gesture to 'a harsh, tragic shadow'.[9] While 'the bewildering fact that each level speaks in the equally-real-or-symbolic terms of the other' leads Hughes to judge the novel to be a raggedly imperfect art of a book, producing a paradox that makes it truly tragic, I would counter that it is precisely this rhetoric of ambivalent contradiction, with both the protective fiction and the traumatic message of psychic fragility simultaneously colouring each other, which makes for Plath's successful deployment of a strategy of cultural performativity. Not the tone of tragic violence or mythic pathos, as in the *Ariel* poems, impresses here, but rather the brilliant eye for the absurd humour inherent to the constrictive scenario of romantic self-absorption and the impasse of scepticism played through in her *Journals* of the same time period. In this novel, which begins with a reference to the death penalty by electric shock imposed on those who do not politically fit the anti-communist world of Eisenhower's America – 'It was a queer, sultry summer, the summer they electrocuted the Rosenbergs' (*BJ* 1) – and ends with the successful shock therapy of a young college student who feels she does not fit in culturally with her peers, Plath's narrative strategy of reiteration produces a fictional world that is both hilariously funny and utterly disconcerting, because it discloses how traumatic shock, far from being located on the other side of the law, actually inhabits these regulative social codes at their very core. In other words, the disconcerting duplicity Plath performs in *The Bell Jar* aims at disclosing how the knowledge of psychic alienation and death urge in fact functions as the shared secret upon which the smooth artificiality, the cool glamour, and the apple-pie happy domesticity proclaimed by 1950s commercial culture came to rest.

As in *The Journals*, the first-person narrator of *The Bell Jar* finds herself in a psychic impasse, seeing her life branch out before her like a green fig tree, yet unable to decide whether to chose the scenario of 'a husband and a happy home and children', or that of public celebrity as a 'famous poet', 'a brilliant professor', an 'amazing editor', that of foreign travel, 'lovers with queer names and off-beat professions', or finally that of 'an Olympic lady crew champion'. But, in contrast to Stanley Dolan's fantasy girl who excels at everything, Esther Greenwood finds her fantasy world rotting before her very eyes owing to her indecision: 'I wanted each and every one of them, but choosing one meant losing all the rest, and, as I sat there, unable to decide, the figs began to wrinkle and go black, and, one by one, they plopped to the ground at my feet' (*BJ* 80). As part of the playfulness of the narrative tone, Esther adds that, once she has satisfied her actual hunger, she is no longer certain whether her vision of the fig tree had not in fact 'arisen from the profound void of an empty stomach' (*BJ* 81), and yet it does serve as a symptom of the psychic dilemma called forth by her internship with a New York fashion magazine, during which, after nineteen years of good marks, prizes, and grants, she is forced to recognize that something is wrong with her because, far from 'having the time of her life' (*BJ* 2), she finds she does not fit into the world whose recognition she so desperately desires, and concomitantly utterly loses her bearings and her ability to control her actions. Part of her disorientation has to do with the fact that she feels ill at ease with the urban dating system, repeatedly involving herself in highly charged sexual scenes, but, because sexual pureness is 'the great issue' (*BJ* 85), she finds herself torn between her desire to lose her virginity and her inability to carry through the promiscuity of her sexually daring friends. She takes on the assumed name Elly Higginbottom when she meets potential lovers, she drops asleep drunk on the bed of the simultaneous translator Constantin, afraid that if she were to realize her fantasy of seduction he would 'sink into ordinariness' (*BJ* 86); she flees from the woman-hater Marco, who assaults her on the lawn during a dance.

The other reason why she comes to believe that far from steering clear into success she is in fact 'dropping clean out of the race' (*BJ* 30) involves her insecurity about whether she is in fact accomplished enough to be a public success. Challenged by the editor of the magazine Jay Cee to explain in what way she feels she is more accomplished than all the other girls who 'flood into New York every June thinking they'll be editors' (*BJ* 35), she begins to fear that she is no more than a fraud, that perhaps she has no real skills but instead has come as far as she has merely owing to false pretences, such as swindling her way through college credits and tricking her benefactress, the novelist Philomena Guinea, into giving her a scholarship. Indeed, the scene in which the last round of photographs of the girls on the internship programme is taken before the issue goes to press comes to summarize how the entire New York episode served to unsettle the psychic distress lurking beneath the happy surface of the all-accomplished self-confident American girl. As she looks for a prop that will represent what she wants to become, Esther, of whom Jay Cee wittily remarks she 'wants to be everything', finally opts for a long-stemmed paper rose to stand for the profession of being a poet, and yet, though asked to smile, the minute the shutter has clicked she breaks into tears. The face she sees in her hand mirror 'seemed to be peering from the grating of a prison cell after a prolonged beating. It was bruised and puffy and all the wrong colours' (*BJ* 107). However, even though Plath's heroine Esther incessantly points to what is amiss in the glamorous New York's fashion world, the tone is not that of despairing, sceptical anguish so often the predominant voice in *The Journals*, but rather one of self-parody and black humour, as in the passage when, having deserted her friend Doreen in the apartment of a disc jockey, she walks forty-three blocks back to her hotel, and, upon finally arriving, ironically comments on the way her physiognomy has taken on her sense of alienation in the course of this nocturnal march. As the elevator doors close, she notes, 'My ears went funny, and I noticed a big, smudgy-eyed Chinese woman staring idiotically into my face. It was only me, of course. I was appalled to see how wrinkled and used-up I looked' (*BJ* 19).

But, if the experience of the fashion world in New York City had suddenly made her sense the toxic side effects of the duplicitous image of the self-assured and successful college student, the home she returns to is from the start encoded as a lethal site: 'the motherly breath of the suburbs enfolded me. It smelt of lawn sprinklers and station-wagons and tennis rackets and dogs and babies. A summer calm laid its soothing hand over everything, like death' (*BJ* 119). Discovering that she has been rejected for the writing course at the Harvard summer school, she suddenly feels thoroughly imprisoned in her mother's house. She exchanges the incapacitating anxiety that she will curtail her opportunities if she decides on one social identity for an indulgence in excessive hysterical *tedium vitae*. Convinced that she has nothing but unchanging repetition to look forward to – with 'day after day after day glaring ahead of me like a white, broad, infinitely desolate avenue' – all action appears meaningless: 'I wanted to do everything once and for all and be through with it' (*BJ* 135). Significantly, her realization that she could not begin to write a novel until she has gained some life-experience, her inability to learn the practical skills of typing and shorthand her mother was teaching with such success to city college girls, as well as her decision to drop her honours programme, indeed the ever more persistent inability to imagine any future for herself at all are clearly linked to her sense that something is as much amiss in the unblemished integrity put to show in this world of motherhood, of honest, unsophisticated domesticity and of practical secretarial work, as in the artificial buzz of New York's publishing world. In earlier chapters she had already disclosed the fiction of the fine, clean suburban college boy, when, discovering from her fiancé Buddy Willard, a medical student at Yale, that he 'had lost his pureness and his virginity' to a waitress the prior summer while he was working as a busboy, she is forced to recognize that their entire relationship, and with it the esteem she gained from her peers as well as her mother and grandmother, was based on hypocrisy. When they discover that Buddy, who had previously been so 'proud of his perfect health', has TB, Esther concludes wryly that this 'might just be a punishment for living the kind of double life Buddy lived and feeling so superior to people' (BJ 75). In the light of her growing conviction that the 'infinite security' of marriage and motherhood is comparable to 'being brainwashed, and afterwards you went about numb as a slave in some private, totalitarian state' (BJ 89), her neighbour, Dodo Conway, suddenly appears like a portentous phantom-figure of the maternal interpellative call towards procreation. Waking up the first morning to the 'soprano screak of carriage wheels', Esther watches the highly pregnant woman wheeling her baby carriage back and forth across the street from her window, followed by three of her other children. Because she imagines that this proud exhibition of maternity – 'A serene, almost religious smile lit up the woman's face. Her head tilted happily back, like a sparrow egg perched on a duck egg, she smiled into the sun' (BJ 122) – was being explicitly staged for her benefit, Esther experiences a bout of anxiety which makes her turn away from the bright light of what she perceives to be duplicitous happiness and engulf herself in the darkness of her pillow, pretending it was night.

Briefly she entertains the thought that she might rewrite her family romance by changing her name, moving to Chicago, and taking on an assumed name. In this fantasy of utter dislocation she would be relieved from the sense of failure so strongly weighing on her current self-image: 'nobody would know I had thrown up a scholarship at a big eastern women's college and mucked up a month in New York and refused a perfectly solid medical student for a husband...I would be simple Elly Higginbottom, the orphan' (*BJ* 140). However, relentlessly caught in a crisis of symbolic investiture, where, finding herself unable to respond to the interpellative call of maternal figures of authority, indeed unable to accept the symbolic mandate they offer her – Jay Cee's offer she become an accomplished magazine editor, her mother's offer she perfect her secretarial skills and write her novel, her mother's friend Mrs Willard's offer she marry her promising young son – Esther in fact experiences a hollowing-out of the symbolic register of possible identities. As a result, any form of professional or domestic achievement seems both fraudulent and lethally repetitive, painfully pointing to the sense of void inhabiting her pose of the Ivy Smith-like successful prize-winning student and poet.[10] Overwhelmed with an anxiety that makes her feel as though she 'were being stuffed farther and farther into a black, airless sack with no way out' (*BJ* 136), a real encounter with death – which is to say a radical form of dislocating herself from accepting any symbolic mandates – emerges as the only viable solution to her psychic dilemma.

The plethora of death plots she designs for herself before she finally takes an overdose of sleeping pills are, of course, linked to her realization of her limitations as an artist. Because she has not been chosen to study with a celebrated author at the same time that her lack of experience prohibits her from writing a novel on her own, Esther indulges herself in a hysterical patchwork of fantasy scenarios ending in death, but, as part of her narrative strategy of cultural reiteration, Plath's parody serves to illustrate that this convoluted fantasy of death, meant as an answer to a psychic impasse, is itself nothing other than an exaggerated materialization at her own body of the popular gothic literature she has read. If her idea of changing her identity to the orphan Elly Higginbottom would entail a social death of sorts, Japanese disembowelment comes to her mind as the first of many concrete ways of self-extinction one could perform 'when everything went wrong' (*BJ* 145), and yet she ends her detailed description of this ritual with the ironic comment, 'It must take a lot of courage to die like that. My trouble was I hated the sight of blood' (*BJ* 146). In the same vein of black humour, Esther compares a snapshot of herself with the newspaper photo of a starlet who died after a sixty-eight-hour coma, only to find that the mouth and nose matched, and that, if the dead girl's eyes were opened, they would have 'the same dead, black, vacant expression as the eyes in the snapshot' (*BJ* 154). Her first unsuccessful experiments with suicide are equally fraught with sprawning reiterations of cultural images of death, for, owing to the comic, self-ironic commentary that accompanies Esther's death speculations, Plath emphasizes the difference between the Esther, whose symbolic universe is slowly caving in, reduced entirely to its inherent void, and the Esther belatedly transforming this experience of psychic dissolution into a narrative, which focuses on the exaggeration and histrionic quality of these death scripts. By thus disclosing how her heroine's fantasies of self-destructions are as much clichés as the stories of feminine success and good living against which they are pitted, Plath undermines the cultural formations on which they depend. The impasse of her heroine's death plot is such that it places Esther between a vast archive of clichéed images of death and the void of real non-existence, utterly outside all symbolization and all fantasy work.

Imagining 'some old Roman philosopher or other', Esther decides to lie in a tub of water and open her veins; however, finding herself unable to cut the white and defenceless wrists, she tries looking in the mirror of the medicine cabinet, so 'it would be like watching somebody else, in a book or a play'. Having thus wasted the entire morning in mere suicidal speculation, Esther fears that her mother will find her before she is done, and is forced to interrupt the entire attempt. Later that day, lying on the beach, she continues to indulge in suicidal fantasies, yet the fact that each scenario leads to an impasse betrays the grotesque core of her fantasy work. She decides that she cannot slit her wrist here because she 'had the razors, but no bath', but renting a room in a boarding house would mean constant interruption by other lodgers (*BJ* 160), while the thought of sharks' teeth and whales' earbones littered at the bottom of the ocean like gravestones leaves her too coward to attempt drowning. Similarly her attempt to hang herself fails because the ceilings in her home are too low, so that she likens the silk cord dangling from her neck to a 'yellow cat's tail', and, because she finds no place to fasten it, she attempts instead to strangle herself, significantly while sitting on her mother's bed. However, she discovers too late that her body has all 'sorts of little tricks' (*BJ* 168) to protect itself, like making her hands go limp in the crucial second. Then again her second attempt at drowning herself in mid-ocean fails, because each time she dives down she pops up again, 'like a cork' (*BJ* 170). She comes to realize that her will to die is repeatedly beaten by circumstantial accidents. Only upon visiting her father's gravestone, and there finding herself crying for the first time for her father's death, does the heroine finally concoct a script that she can pit against her mother's resilient plot of survival, indeed implicitly ascribing to her a refusal to mourn, inspired by the Nazi ideology of euthanasia: 'She had just smiled and said what a merciful thing it was for him he had died, because if he had lived he would have been crippled and an invalid for life, and he couldn't have stood that, he would rather have died than had that happen'. Under the auspices of her father's name, graved in stone, she comes up with a feasible plan: 'I knew just how to go about it' (*BJ* 177).

Even if the perepeteia to Esther's suicidal script borrows more from the melodramatic tone of the sentimental woman's films, whose screen plays were adaptations of novels such as those written by her benefactress, Plath's description of her heroine taking an overdose of sleeping tablets in the basement of her mother's home reintroduces the grotesque gothic element. Emphasizing the discrepancy between Esther's desire to 'do things in a calm, orderly way' and the fact that she actually finds it quite difficult to fit her body into a gap in the wall, the narratorial voice commenting on this scene retrospectively describes her former self, waiting for death, as one 'crouched at the mouth of the darkness, like a troll' (*BJ* 179). Part of Plath's strategy of cultural performativity, furthermore, resides in the fact that even this enactment, undertaken in response to a mandate implicitly given to her by her dead father, fails. Unable to find the pathos-filled tragic end the literature of high culture dictates, Esther, after experiencing a soothing sleep-like vision-less and soundless darkness, finds herself back in the plot of mass-market women's fiction, and quite concretely in her mother's suburban world. Indeed, the first thing she hears as she slowly gains back her senses, is her own voice, calling 'Mother!' (*BJ* 181).

Esther's mental and social process of recuperation in part entails defining herself in relation to masculine lovers, on the one hand, by separating from her fiancé Buddy Willard and the duplicity this relation had come to signify for her, and, on the other, by having an affair with a well-paid professor of mathematics at Harvard so as finally to succeed in losing her virginity, of which she says it 'weighed like a millstone around my neck'. Once more her actions appear like reiterations of texts read, for she claims she wanted to commit this significant act with 'somebody I didn't know and wouldn't go on knowing – a kind of impersonal, priestlike official, as in the tales of tribal rites' (*BJ* 240). In both cases, gaining an independent sexual identity also involves rejecting the option of lesbian love presented to her in the figure of Joan, who, having read about her suicide, decided to imitate her, only to end up in the same clinic. Joan had also been dating Billy, and it is while Joan and Esther are living together in Boston that Esther has her first heterosexual experience. And yet Esther's restitution significantly occurs above all under the auspices of two maternal figures, her benefactress, Philomena Guinea, who is willing to pay for her treatment at a private because, 'at the peak of her career, she had been in an asylum as well' (*BJ* 195), and her therapist, Dr Nolan, who patiently helps her overcome her paranoid fantasies and suicidal urges, symbolized in the image of the bell jar, cutting off all circulation from the outside world and forcing her to stew in her own sour air. Ultimately she succeeds in her therapy precisely because she is able to teach Esther to establish a relationship of trust and reliability with her as a surrogate maternal figure of authority at the same time as she allows her patient to voice her hatred for her real mother. Seeking to counteract the guilt the maternal interpellative gaze evokes in Esther, who belatedly recalls, 'My mother was the worst. She never scolded me, but kept begging me, with a sorrowful face, to tell her what she had done wrong,' (*BJ* 215), Dr Nolan terminates all further visits from relatives and friends.

Nevertheless, even while Esther recovers, her awareness of the presence of death in the midst of life remains with her.

Being driven in the car of her benefactress to the private clinic, for example, she fantasizes that, as they are passing over a bridge, she might fling herself out of the car and into the river below them, but, because she is wedged in between her mother and her brother, when she moves forward, each lays a hand on the door handle. With the same self-irony that the narrator used to comment on the earlier failed suicide attempts, she now notes, 'I missed a perfectly good chance' (BJ 197). Along the same lines her defloration, resulting in a haemorrhage, is also connected first with 'the stories of blood-stained bridal sheets and capsules of red ink bestowed on already deflowered brides' (BJ 242), and then, when her pains persist, with images of fatality she remembers from Victorian novels 'where woman after woman died, palely and nobly, in torrents of blood, after a difficult childbirth' (BJ 244), only to be told by the doctor that her anatomical abnormality can be fixed. Even after her six-month therapy at the clinic promises to be successful and the bell jar appears to be fully suspended above her head, she cannot obey her mother's wish to act as if her suicide attempt and her stay at the clinic 'were a bad dream'. Instead, she insists that the cracks on the surface of personal health and happiness be acknowledged, because, only too aware that she can remember everything about her breakdown, she knows that the traces of this nightmare will continue to haunt her: 'they were part of me. They were my landscape' (BJ 250). Indeed one of the toxic side issues to her own recuperation is that Joan succeeds in running away from the clinic and hanging herself in the nearby woods. Standing at her friend's grave, Esther can finally assure herself that she has regained a stable sense of identity: 'I took a deep breath and listened to the old brag of my heart. I, I, I' (BJ 256). With this statement she chiasmically puts closure on her urge for self-dissolution which she felt the day she was at the beach when she first came to contemplate the Virginia Woolf-inspired death by drowning: 'As I paddled on, my heartbeat boomed like a dull motor in my ears. I am I am I am' (BJ 167). It is as if, belatedly reiterating the contingent events of her psychic anguish in the form of a narrative about having gone through madness and near death and returned to the living, she were able to construct the imaginary home she can now successfully locate herself in.

This final staging of Esther's ritual of being born a second time, with the heroine now seemingly comfortable with the contradictions of life, able to live the commas separating her various identities rather than expending herself in a whirlpool of choices and expectations, of course, reads like a reiteration of the happy end of Hollywood melodramas, and, as Ted Hughes convincingly points out, the protective positive resolution troubles the traumatic material that has been brought to the fore. I would simply add that this discrepancy need not be read as an aesthetic failure, but rather as an entirely successful strategy on the part of Plath aimed at pointing out to her readers that we cannot have the fiction of apple-pie happiness without some real worms in it. Indeed, she dismantles the very closure her narrative rests upon precisely because, throughout her novel, she has performed fantasy scenarios for us that illustrate why we must distrust any surface representation that shows a seemingly intact picture. In one of the funniest scenes of the novel, Esther describes her invitation to a banquet sponsored by *Ladies' Day*, 'the big women's magazine that features lush double-page spreads of technicolour meals' (*BJ* 24). Arrayed on the banquet table Esther finds her favourite foods, 'avocado pear halves stuffed with crabmeat and mayonnaise, and platters of rare roast beef and cold chicken, and every so often a cut-glass bowl heaped with black caviar' (*BJ* 25). Already feeling dizzy owing to the sight of all the food stacks in the magazine kitchen they had toured, witnessing how difficult it is to produce the glossy images of food photography, Esther grows quite reckless in her effort to eat as much of the caviar she can before moving on to the crabmeat. Then, finding herself herded off to a cinema to watch a football romance in technicolour, she begins to feel peculiar at precisely the moment she recognizes that the 'nice girl was going to end up with the nice football hero and the sexy girl was going to end up with nobody', though as of yet unsure whether 'it was the awful movie giving me a stomach-ache or all that caviar I had eaten' (*BJ* 44). As it turns out, the entire group of college women was poisoned by the crabmeat, which tests show was full of ptomaine. As she thinks about this collective poisoning, Esther hallucinates the scene during which the cover photograph for the next issue of the magazine is being produced. In this fantasy scene, surface glamour and hidden destruction are so perfectly welded together that no one will be able to tell the toxic elements contained in the perfect image: 'I had a vision of the celestially white kitchens on *Ladies' Day* stretching into infinity. I saw avocado pear after avocado pear being stuffed with crabmeat and mayonnaise and photographed under brilliant lights. I saw the delicate, pink-mottled claw-meat poking seductively through its blanket of mayonnaise and the bland yellow pear cup with its rim of alligator-green cradling the whole mess' (*BJ* 50).

Reading *The Bell Jar* more than a quarter of a century after it was initially published, we can perhaps more fully enjoy the black humour contained in a text in which, by virtue of the rhetoric of horrific exaggeration, the lethal quality of a celebration of artificiality breaks through the glamorous surface. Initially Plath's novel had been acclaimed above all as a feminist manifesto *avant la lettre* and praised for the way it relentlessly uncovers the double standard of rules of chastity imposed on women growing up in the 1950s, the trap that the promised happiness of suburban marriage and motherhood could turn into for college-educated women, indeed the impossibility of fulfilling the role of the accomplished professional woman, who is successful in everything she does. On the other side of the sexual revolution, the women's movement, the civil-rights movement, the cold war, and *glasnost*, which is to say in a world that speaks of global communities, crossover identities and cultural hybridity, we can now perhaps come to value *The Bell Jar* for its astonishingly astute depiction of two aspects of postmodernity. By emphasizing how inextricably linked her heroine's self-identity is with the products of contemporary popular culture, to the extent that the disclosed toxic remains, supposedly excluded from any happy self-image, cannot in fact be distinguished from the cleaned artificial surface, Plath offers us an utterly compelling representation of how, in the highly commercialized and media infiltrated culture of the late twentieth century Western world, we are the signs we consume even while we are consumed by them.[11] Furthermore, in the light of the political unrest that has begun to emerge as a fifty-years after effect, given that the opening of the archives pertaining to all the shared secrets upon which post-Second World War prosperity was based means confronting the remains preserved in our collective cultural crypt, Plath's insistence that clandestine traumatic knowledge not only always haunts its host but will strike back and shatter protective fictions of infallibility with a force equal to the effort put into repressing this truth suddenly seems uncannily pertinent. In hindsight, the Ivy Smith girl who can do everything with a clean bright smile on her face is in fact a horrific monster, because we cannot help but sense the forces of destruction lurking beneath the duplicitous surface of utterly perfect artificiality.

Notes

CHAPTER 1. THE PLATH MYTH

1. The letter by Julia Parnaby and Rachel Wingfield was published in the *Guardian* on 7 April 1989 under the title 'In Memory of Sylvia Plath'. A. Alvarez's letter, co-signed by Joseph Brodsky, Helga Graham, Ronald Hayman, Jill Neville, Peter Orr, Peter Porter, and John Carey, appeared on 11 April. Ruth Richardson's, A. B. Ewen's, and William Park's letters appeared on 12 April. On 13 April Parnaby and Wingfield responded to their critics, while Margaret Drabble offered her criticism. On 15 April John Harrison, Vicar of Heptonstall, presented his view of the case. Ted Hughes's letter to the publisher was published in the *Guardian* on 20 April, and on 26 April Parnaby and Wingfield's final response was printed.
2. See Robert Lowell's foreword to the American edition of *Ariel* (New York: Harper & Rowe, 1961), p. vii.
3. See Roland Barthes, 'Myth Today', in *A Barthes Reader*, ed. Susan Sontag (New York: Hill & Wang, 1982), 104.
4. See Sigmund Freud, 'Fetishism', initially published in 1927 (Standard Edition, 21; London: Hogarth Press, 1961), 149–57.
5. See Jean-Pierre Vernant, 'Figuration de l'invisible et catégorie psychologique du double: Le Colossus', in Vernant, *Mythe & pensée chez les Grecs* (Paris: La Découverte, 1988), 325–38.
6. See Roland Barthes's autobiographical texts *Roland Barthes* (New York: Hill & Wang, 1977), 90.
7. See Jacqueline Rose, *The Haunting of Sylvia Plath* (London: Virago Press, 1991), 69.
8. Leo Braudy, *The Frenzy of Renown: Fame and its History* (New York/ Oxford: Oxford University Press, 1986), 542.
9. See Ted Hughes, 'Sylvia Plath and her Journals', first published in *Grand Street* in 1982 and repr. in *Winter Pollen: Occasional Prose*, ed. William Scammell (New York: Picador, 1994), 177.
10. Ibid. 188.

11. Ibid. 189.
12. A. Alvarez, *The Savage God: A Study of Suicide* (Harmondsworth: Penguin, 1974), 26, 40.
13. Ibid. 55.
14. Janet Malcolm, *The Silent Woman: Sylvia Plath & Ted Hughes* (New York: Alfred Knopf, 1994), 66.
15. Rose, *The Haunting*, 73.
16. Ellen Moers, *Literary Women: The Great Writers* (New York: Doubleday, 1977), p. xviii.
17. Sandra M. Gilbert, ' "A Fine, White Flying Myth": Confessions of a Plath Addict', first published in the *Massachusetts Review* in 1978, and repr. in Harold Bloom (ed.), *Sylvia Plath* (New York: Chelsea House Publishers, 1989), 49–65.
18. Ibid. 55.
19. See Linda W. Wagner (ed.), *Critical Essays on Sylvia Plath* (Boston: G. K. Hall, 1984), 1–24.
20. Harold Fromm, 'Sylvia Plath, Hunger Artist', *Hudson Review*, 43/2 (Summer 1990), 254.
21. Anne Stevenson, 'Sylvia Plath and the Romantic Heritage', *PN Review*, 16/6 (1990), 20.
22. Ibid. 21.
23. George Steiner, 'Dying is an Art', in Steiner, *Language and Silence* (London: Faber & Faber, 1967), 329.
24. Marjorie G. Perloff, 'On the Road to Ariel: The "Transitional" Poetry of Sylvia Plath', in Edward Butscher (ed.), *Sylvia Plath: The Woman and the Work* (New York: Dodd, Mead, 1977), 142.
25. Irwing Howe, 'The Plath Celebration: A Partial Dissent', in Bloom (ed.), *Sylvia Plath*, 13.
26. Elizabeth Hardwick, 'On Sylvia Plath', in Paul Alexander (ed.), *Ariel Ascending: Writings about Sylvia Plath* (New York: Harper & Row, 1985), 102.
27. Ibid. 112.
28. Katha Pollitt, 'A Note of Triumph: On *The Collected Poems*', in Alexander (ed.), *Ariel Ascending*, 96.
29. Bruce Bawer, 'Sylvia Plath and the Poetry of Confession', *New Criterion*, 9/6 (1991), 19.
30. Ibid. 23–6 *passim*.
31. Malcolm, *Silent Woman*, 58.
32. Articles from this issue were republished in 1970 along with other scholarly and biographical texts, as well as writings by Plath that up to that point had never been published, as Charles Newman (ed.), *The Art of Sylvia Plath: A Symposium* (Bloomington, Ind.: Indiana University Press, 1970).
33. Anne Stevenson, *Bitter Fame: A Life of Sylvia Plath* (New York: Viking,

1989), p. ix.
34. See Mary Lynn Broe, 'Pathologies: The "Blood Jet" Is Bucks, not Poetry', *Belles Lettres*, 10/1 (Fall 1994), 50–1 *passim*.
35. Rose, *The Haunting*, 2.
36. Ibid. 8.
37. Ibid. 76.
38. Ibid. 104.
39. Malcolm, *Silent Woman*, 176.
40. Ibid. 17.
41. Barbara Johnson, 'Apostrophe, Animation, and Abortion', in Johnson, *A World of Difference* (Baltimore: Johns Hopkins University Press, 1987), 185.
42. Ted Hughes, *Birthday Letters* (London: Faber & Faber, 1998), 17.
43. Ibid. 193.
44. Ibid. 15, 24.
45. Ibid. 139.
46. Ibid. 68.
47 Andrew Motion, 'A Thunderbolt from the Blue: This Book Will Live Forever', *The Times* 17 January 1988, p. 22.
48. Sarah Lyall, 'A Divided Response of Hughes Poems', *New York Times*, Arts Page, 17 January 1988, pp. 1, 7.
49. See Nicolas Abraham and Maria Torok 'The Topography of Reality: Sketching a Metapsychology of Secrets', in Abraham and Torok, *The Shell and the Kernel*, i, ed. and trans. Nicholas T. Rand (Chicago: University of Chicago Press, 1994), 158.

CHAPTER 2.   THE AUTOBIOGRAPHICAL WRITINGS

1. Ted Hughes, 'Sylvia Plath and her Journals' in *Winter Pollen: Occasional Prose*, ed. William Scammell (New York: Picador, 1994), 178.
2. Janet Malcolm, *The Silent Woman: Sylvia Plath & Ted Hughes* (New York: Alfred Knopf, 1994), 155–6 *passim*.
3. Ibid. 96.
4. Ibid. 100.
5. See Stanley Cavell's compelling reading of Shakespeare's Othello, 'The Stake of the Other', in *Disowning Knowledge in Six Plays of Shakespeare* (Cambridge: Cambridge University Press, 1987, 125–42).
6. Sylvia Plath turned this event into the subject of her story 'Stone Boy with Dolphin', part of the stories collected at the Lilly Library and published posthumously in *JP*, a collection of prose writings put together by Ted Hughes.
7. Nicolas Abraham and Maria Torok, *The Shell and the Kernel*, i, ed. and

trans. Nicholas T. Rand (Chicago: University of Chicago Press, 1994), especially the article 'Notes on the Phantom: A Complement to Freud's Metapsychology', 171–6.

8. For an overview of the discussion of hysteria, see Ilza Veith's *Hysteria: The History of a Disease* (Chicago: University of Chicago Press, 1965), and Elaine Showalter's, *The Female Malady: Women, Madness, and English Culture, 1830–1980* (New York: Pantheon Books, 1985).

9. In 'Pursuit', in *CP*, 22–3, a poem not included in *Col*. Plath offers a poetic rendition of the early phase of her relationship with Hughes, comparing him to a black marauding panther, stalking her down, snaring her with his ardour. Although she seeks to flee from her own lust, she finds him following her up the stairs into the sanctuary of her private rooms. In a much later poem, 'The Rabbit Catcher', (*CP* 193–4), which although she had wanted to include it in *Ariel* was left out of the edition Ted Hughes finally published, Plath returns to a fantasy where violence and erotic desire are inextricably enmeshed. As she shifts from describing her excitement at being the object of nature's overpowering force to the excitement of the hunter, waiting for his prey, she compares herself to the rabbit caught in her lover's killing snares.

10. Fully in line with the gothic mode in which the entire episode is written, the rhododendrons recall the flowers associated with the sexually dangerous wife of Maxim de Winter in Daphne du Maurier's *Rebecca* initially published 1938 (London: Pan Books, 1975), against whom the heroine must assert her own chaste behaviour to win the love of her murderer-husband.

11. See Jacques Lacan, 'Intervention on Transference', originally published in 1951 and repr. in Charles Bernheimer and Claire Kahane *In Dora's Case: Freud–Hysteria–Feminism* (Ithaca: Cornell University Press, 1985), 92–104.

12. See Jacques Lacan, 'On a Question Preliminary to any Possible Treatment of Psychosis', repr. in Lacan, *Écrits: A Selection*, ed. Alan Sheridan (New York: Norton, 1977), summarizing the work of his seminar during 1955–6, p. 194.

13. Slavoj Zizek, *The Indivisible Remainder: An Essay on Schelling and Related Matters* (London: Verso, 1996), 164.

14. Ibid. 165.

15. Malcolm, *Silent Woman*, 16.

16. Ibid. 100.

CHAPTER 3.   THE POEMS

1. See Peter Orr's interview with Sylvia Plath, 30 October 1962, in Orr

(ed.), *The Poet Speaks* (London: Routledge & Kegan Paul, 1966), 169.

2. See Mary Lynn Broe, *Protean Poetic: The Poetry of Sylvia Plath* (Columbia: University of Missouri Press, 1980), 190.

3. Katha Pollitt, 'A Note of Triumph: On the Collected Poems', in Paul Alexander (ed.), *Ariel Ascending: Writers about Sylvia Plath* (New York: Harper & Row, 1985), 98.

4. Sandra M. Gilbert, ' "A Fine, White Flying Myth"': Confessions of a Plath Addict', in Harold Bloom (ed.), *Sylvia Plath* (New York: Chelsea House Publishers, 1989), 57.

5. Richard Allen Blessing, 'The Shape of the Psyche: Vision and Technique in the Late Poems of Sylvia Plath', in Gary Lane (ed.), *Sylvia Plath: New Views on the Poetry* (Baltimore: Johns Hopkins University Press, 1979), 59.

6. See Alicia Ostriker, 'The Americanization of Sylvia', in Ostriker, *Writing Like a Woman* (Ann Arbor, Mich.: University of Michigan Press, 1983), 45.

7. Ibid. 47.

8. Ibid. 52.

9. Orr, *The Poet Speaks*, 170.

10. Ibid. 168.

11. Jacqueline Rose, *The Haunting of Sylvia Plath* (London: Virago Press, 1991), 132.

12. For a psychoanalytically informed discussion of the way Plath's theme of suicidal urge and rebirth is cast within the context of her poetic reworking of the family, see Murray M. Schwartz and Christopher Bollas, 'The Absence at the Center: Sylvia Plath and Suicide' in Lane (ed.), *Sylvia Plath*, 179–202.

13. See Barbara Johnson, 'Apostrophe, Animation, and Abortion', in Johnson, *A World of Difference* (Baltimore: Johns Hopkins University Press, 1987), 188.

14. See Jean-Pierre Vernant, 'Figuration de l'invisible et catégories psychologique du double: Le Colossus', in Vernant, *Mythe & pensée chez les Grecs* (Paris: La Découverte, 1988), 327.

15. See Paul de Man, 'Autobiography as De-Facement', in de Man, *The Rhetoric of Romanticism* (New York: Columbia University Press, 1984), 78.

16. Defending Plath against the criticism that her usage of holocaust imagery to describe her private anguish is utterly inappropriate, James E. Young (*Writing and Rewriting the Holocaust: Narrative and the Consequences of Interpretation* (Bloomington, Ind.: Indiana University Press, 1988), suggests that the reciprocal exchange between outer and inner realities that her late poems stage, in the course of which she came simultaneously to represent her own unhappiness and the situation of political victimhood, in fact points to 'a compelling

131

parallel between "confessional poetry" and the testimonial mode of Holocaust literature: for what is confessional poetry if not that which emphasizes its personal authenticity and link to material over all else.' Along the lines I am suggesting, Young suggests relinquishing the critical dispute over whether there is any authentic reference to her figuration of the holocaust, and looking instead at the way the holocaust, having entered public consciousness as a trope, 'informs both the poet's view of the world and her representations of it in verse', (p. 132). For a discussion of Plath's identification with the Jewish disaster during the holocaust, see also Jacqueline Rose, 'Daddy' in *The Haunting*, 205–38.

17. See Maurice Blanchot's 'Literature and the Right to Death', in Blanchet, *The Gaze of Orpheus and Other Literary Essays*, trans. Lydia Davis (Barrytown: Station Hill Press, 1981), 46. For a discussion of the way death serves as the measure towards but also against which literature is positioned, see Michel Foucault, 'Language to Infinity', in Foucault', *Language, Counter-memory, Practice: Selected Essays and Interviews*, ed. and trans. Donald F. Bouchard, with Sherry Simon (Ithaca, NY: Cornell University Press, 1977), 53–67.

18. Blanchot, 'Literature and the Right to Death', 55.

19. For a discussion of Julia Kristeva's distinction between the symbolic and the semiotic registers of the psyche, see *Revolution in Poetic Language*, trans. Margaret Waller (New York: Columbia University Press, 1984). For her compelling discussion of the abject, see *Powers of Horror: An Essay on Abjection*, trans. Leon S. Roudiez (New York: Columbia University Press, 1982).

20. Joyce C. Oates, 'The Death Throes of Romanticism: The Poetry of Sylvia Plath', in Edward Butscher (ed.), *Sylvia Plath: The Woman and the Work*, (New York: Dodd, Mead, 1977), 210.

21. Rose, *The Haunting*, 149.

22. See Slavoj Zizek's discussion of symbolic death in the films of Roberto Rosellini, in *Enjoy Your Symptoms: Jacques Lacan in Hollywood and out* (New York: Routledge, 1992), 43.

CHAPTER 4. THE PROSE WRITINGS

1. Janet Malcolm, *The Silent Woman: Sylvia Plath & Ted Hughes* (New York: Alfred Knopf, 1994), 16.

2. See the excellent discussion of Plath's debt to the very commercial mass-market culture she also tried to detach herself from by moving to England in Jacqueline Rose, *The Haunting of Sylvia Plath* (London: Virago Press, 1991), 165–204.

3. Judith Butler, *Bodies that Matter: On the Discursive Limits of 'Sex'* (New

York: Routledge, 1993), 2. For a discussion of the question of performativity and reiteration especially in relation to representations of femininity in Western culture, see also Teresa de Lauretis, *Alice Doesn't: Feminism, Semiotics, Cinema* (Bloomington, Ind.; Indiana University Press, 1984), and Luce Irigaray's *Speculum of the Other Woman*, trans. Gillian Gill (Ithaca, NY: Cornell University Press, 1985).

4. Linda W. Wagner, 'Sylvia Plath's Specialness in her Short Stories', *Journal of Narrative Technique*, 15 (Winter 1985), 11.

5. This passage from Sylvia Plath's journals, recording the time period 12 December 1958–15 November 1959, now located at the Sylvia Plath Collection at Smith College Library Rare Book Room, is cited in Rose, *The Haunting*, 272.

6. Ibid, 200.

7. For a discussion of the publication history, see the foreword by Frances McCullough to a re-edition of *The Bell Jar* (New York: HarperCollins, 1996), p. xviii.

8. Rose, *The Haunting*, 186. See also Marilyn Yalom, 'Sylvia Plath, *The Bell Jar*, and Related Poems', in Diane Wood Middlebrook and Marilyn Yalom (eds.), *Coming to Light: American Women Poets in the Twentieth Century* (Ann Arbor, Mich.: University of Michigan Press, 1985), in which she notes that 'one of the little-noticed ironies of *The Bell Jar* is that it is the mother–daughter bond which represents the life force and the father–daughter bond that represents the death force – ironic because mother is the target of such venomous satire and father the recipient of daughterly nostalgia' (p. 179).

9. See Ted Hughes's introduction to a proposed edition of Plath's novel and poetry collected in one volume, 'Sylvia Plath's *Collected Poems* and *The Bell Jar*', in Hughes, *Winter Pollen: Occasional Prose*, ed. William Scammell (New York: Picador, 1994), 480.

10. For a discussion of hysteria and paranoia as responses to crisis in symbolic investiture, see Eric L. Santner's compelling study *My Own Private Germany: Daniel Paul Schreber's Secret History of Modernity* (Princeton: Princeton University Press, 1996).

11. In her review of a new translation of *The Bell Jar* into German, 'Das Leben: Ein hektisches Dabeigewesensein', *Die Zeit*, 15 (4 Apr. 1997), 53, Gisela von Wysocki, noting that translations in general age more quickly than the original texts because they conform to the codes of taste of a given time, praises the new edition for having abandoned the earlier portentous, hopeless tone in favour of an artificial, poetic precision that highlights the manner in which, by caricaturing the world whose duplicity Plath seeks to dismantle, she has produced an artificial world *par excellence*.

Select Bibliography

BIBLIOGRAPHIES AND WORKS BY AND ABOUT PLATH

Northhouse, Cameron, and Walsh, Thomas P., *Sylvia Plath and Anne Sexton: A Reference Guide* (Boston: G. D. Hall & Co., 1974).
Tabor, Stephen, *Sylvia Plath: An Analytic Bibliography* (London/New York: Mansell Publishing, 1986).

WORKS BY SYLVIA PLATH

The Colossus and Other Poems (London: Heinemann, 1960; New York: Alfred Knopf, 1962).
The Bell Jar, by 'Victoria Lucas' (London: Heinemann, 1963); by Sylvia Plath (London: Faber & Faber, 1966; New York: Harper & Row, 1971).
Ariel (London: Faber & Faber, 1965; New York: Harper & Row, 1966).
Crossing the Water (London: Faber & Faber, 1971; New York: Harper & Row, 1972).
Winter Trees (London: Faber & Faber, 1971; New York: Harper & Row, 1972).
Letters Home: Correspondence 1950–1963, selected and edited with a commentary by Aurelia Schober Plath (London: Faber & Faber, 1975; New York: Harper & Row, 1975).
The Bed Book (London: Faber & Faber, 1976; New York: Harper & Row, 1976).
Johnny Panic and the Bible of Dreams: Short Stories, Prose, and Diary Excerpts edited and introduction by Ted Hughes (London: Faber & Faber, 1977; New York: Harper & Row, 1980).
The Collected Poems, edited with an introduction by Ted Hughes (London: Faber & Faber, 1981; New York: Harper & Row, 1981).
The Journals of Sylvia Plath, ed. Frances McCullough, consulting ed. Ted Hughes (New York: Random House (Ballantine Press), 1982).
The It-Doesn't-Matter Suit (London: Faber & Faber, 1996; New York: Harper & Row, 1996).

BIOGRAPHICAL AND CRITICAL STUDIES

Collections of Essays

Alexander, Paul, *Ariel Ascending: Writings about Sylvia Plath* (New York: Harper & Row, 1985). A useful collection of texts on Plath, including both scholarly essays and recollections by family members and friends.

Bloom, Harold, *Sylvia Plath* (New York: Chelsea House Publishers, 1989). A collection of essays which is especially useful because it presents a wide range of scholarly positions from some highly critical to other extremely appreciative voices.

Butscher, Edward, *Sylvia Plath: The Woman and the Work* (New York: Dodd, Mead, 1977). A useful collection of scholarly essays on the biography and the work of Sylvia Plath.

Lane, Gary, *Sylvia Plath: New Views on the Poetry* (Baltimore: Johns Hopkins University Press, 1979). A useful collection of scholarly essays exploring both the aesthetic value as well as the influence of Plath's poetry.

Newman, Charles, ed., *The Art of Sylvia Plath: A Symposium* (Bloomington, Ind., Indiana University Press, 1970). An insightful expanded edition of articles published in a special commemorative issue of *Tri-Quarterly* in 1966, including both biographical essays on Plath as well as texts offering a scholarly discussion of her themes and prosody as well as an appendix with material that was at the time unpublished.

Wagner, Linda W., *Critical Essays on Sylvia Plath* (Boston: G. K. Hall, 1984). A useful collection of essays including reviews of Plath's writing as well as scholarly essays, with particular emphasis on feminist criticism of her work.

Individual Books and Essays

Aird, Eileen, *Sylvia Plath* (New York: Barnes & Nobles, 1973). The first monograph offering a comprehensive reading of Plath's work.

Alvarez, A., *The Savage God: A Study of Suicide* (Harmondsworth: Penguin, 1974). In the prologue to this study Alvarez offers his personal recollection of Sylvia Plath and praises her as one of the outstanding voices in contemporary British/American poetry.

Banerjee, Jacqueline, 'Grief and the Modern Writer', *English: The Journal of the English Association*, 43 (1994), 17–36. A discussion of Plath's writings in the context of the work of mourning.

Bawer, Bruce, 'Sylvia Plath and the Poetry of Confession' *New Criterion*, 9/6 (1991), 18–27. An insightful though highly critical discussion of Plath's work in the context of reviewing Anne Stevenson's biography *Bitter Fame*.

Blessing, Richard Allen, *The Shape of the Psyche: Vision and Technique in the*

Late Poems of Sylvia Plath, in Gary Lane (ed.), *Sylvia Plath: New Views on the Poetry* (Baltimore: Johns Hopkins University Press, 1979), 57–73. An article focusing on Plath as an escape artist.

Broe, Mary Lynn, *Protean Poetic: The Poetry of Sylvia Plath* (Columbia: University of Missouri Press, 1980). An insightful study of Plath's work, focusing on the manner in which she came to construct a plethora of poetic self-images.

—— 'Pathologies: The "Blood Jet" is Bucks, not Poetry', *Belles Lettres*, 10/1 (Fall 1994), 49-62. A spirited critic of recent biographies and scholarly publications on Plath.

Bundtzen, Lynda K., *Plath's Incarnations: Women and the Creative Process* (Ann Arbor, Mich.: University of Michigan Press, 1983). A useful study focusing on the question of gender and creativity in Plath's work.

Butscher, Edward, *Sylvia Plath: Method and Madness* (New York: Seabury Press, 1976). A biography, emphasizing the multiple roles Plath came to perfect during her lifetime.

Dickie, Margaret, 'Seeing is Re-Seeing: Sylvia Plath and Elizabeth Bishop', *American Literature*, 65/1 (1993), 131–46. Dickie offers a fresh reading of Plath's poem 'The Beekeeper's Daughter' in conjunction with Julia Kristeva's writings on the abject.

Fromm, Harold, 'Sylvia Plath, Hunger Artist', *Hudson Review*, 43/2 (Summer 1990), 245–56. A useful review of Anne Stevenson's biography.

Gilbert, Sandra M., ' "A Fine, White Flying Myth": Confessions of a Plath Addict', in Harold Bloom (ed.), *Sylvia Plath* (New York: Chelsea House Publishers, 1989), 49–65. An insightful discussion of the theme of enclosure and freedom in Plath's writings.

—— , and Gubar, Susan, *The Madwoman in the Attic: The Woman Writer and the Nineteenth Century Literary Imagination* (New Haven: Yale University Press, 1979). Discusses Sylvia Plath in the context of feminine plots developed by women writing in the nineteenth century.

—— No Man's Land: The Place of the Woman Writer in the Twentieth Century, iii *Letters from the Front* (New Haven: Yale University Press, 1994). Focuses primarily on the manner in which Plath addresses the issue of rage, violence, battle, anger, and competition in her writings.

Hampl, Patricia, 'The Smile of Accomplishment: Sylvia Plath's Ambition', *Iowa Review*, 25/1 (1995), 1–28. Hampl discusses the feminist implications of Plath's mythic vision of self-transformation and its relation to death.

Hardwick, Elizabeth, 'On Sylvia Plath', in Paul Alexander (ed.), *Ariel Ascending: Writings about Sylvia Plath* (New York: Harper & Row, 1985), 100–15. In this compelling article Hardwick praises Plath's work for its resilience and refusal to give in to conventions.

Holbrook, David, *Sylvia Plath: Poetry and Existence* (London: Athlone Press, 1976). A highly reductive reading of Sylvia Plath as a schizophrenic author.

Howe, Irving, 'The Plath Celebration: A Partial Dissent', in Harold Bloom (ed.), *Sylvia Plath* (New York: Chelsea House Publishers, 1989), 5–15. A critical discussion of Plath's use of holocaust imagery in her late poetry.

Hughes, Ted, 'Sylvia Plath and her Journals', in Hughes, *Winter Pollen: Occasional Prose*, ed. William Scammell (New York: Picador, 1994), 177–90. Hughes offers an insightful personal recollection of the relation between Sylvia Plath's development as a poet and her autobiographical writings.

—— 'Sylvia Plath: The Evolution of "Sheep in Fog"', in Hughes, *Winter Pollen: Occasional Prose*, ed. William Scammell (New York: Picador, 1994), 191–211. Hughes uses a close reading of the changes Plath undertook as she rewrote this poem to discuss the turning point in Plath's artistic style.

—— 'Sylvia Plath's *Collected Poems* and *The Bell Jar*', in Hughes, *Winter Pollen: Occasional Prose*, ed. William Scammell (New York: Picador, 1994), 466–81. Hughes contrasts Plath's late poetry to her novel and discusses all her writing as a battle between her authentic self and the false selves she came to assume.

—— *Birthday Letters* (London: Faber & Faber, 1998).

Kroll, Judith, *Chapters in a Mythology: The Poetry of Sylvia Plath* (New York: Harper & Row, 1976). An early study on Plath's work in the context of her reworking of mythological scenes.

Lant, Kathleen Margaret, 'The Big Strip Tease: Female Bodies and Male Power in the Poetry of Sylvia Plath', *Contemporary Literature*, 34/4 (1993), 620–69. An astute discussion of the gender constructions underlying Plath's thematization of creative powers, which involves both her appropriation of masculinity for her notion of her own poetic self-image as well as her rejection of paternal figures of authority.

Lowell, Robert, Preface to *Ariel* (New York: Harper & Row, 1966). Important as one of the first comments on Sylvia Plath as a confessional poet.

Malcolm, Janet, *The Silent Woman: Sylvia Plath & Ted Hughes* (New York: Alfred Knopf, 1994). An excellent discussion of what has been at stake in the diverse biographies and critical studies of Sylvia Plath.

Oates, Joyce C., 'The Death-Throes of Romanticism: The Poetry of Sylvia Plath', in Edward Butscher (ed.), *Sylvia Plath: The Woman and the Work* (New York: Dodd, Mead, 1977), 206–24. A fascinating discussion of Plath's work in context of romantic imagination.

Orr, Peter, *The Poet Speaks* (London: Routledge & Kegan Paul, 1966). Contains a useful late interview with Sylvia Plath.

Ostriker, Alicia, *Writing Like a Woman* (Ann Arbor, Mich.: University of Michigan Press, 1983). In her chapter on Plath, Ostriker reads Plath's late work primarily as a poetic refiguration of her experience of American culture.

Perloff, Marjorie G., 'On the Road to Ariel: The "Transitional" Poetry of Sylvia Plath', in Edward Butscher (ed.), *Sylvia Plath: The Woman and the Work* (New York: Dodd, Mead, 1977), 125–42. An insightful discussion of the various styles of Plath's poetic voice.

—— 'Sylvia Plath's "Sivvy" Poems: A Portrait of the Poet as Daughter', in Gary Lane (ed.), *Sylvia Plath: New Views on the Poetry* (Baltimore: Johns Hopkins University Press, 1979), 155–78. A discussion of the way Plath's poetry addresses the daughter–mother relationship.

—— 'The Two Ariels: The (Re)making of the Sylvia Plath Canon', *American Poetry Review*, 13 (1984), 10–18. Perloff offers a precise comparison between the version of *Ariel* Hughes ultimately published and the one Plath had originally planned before her suicide.

Pollitt, Katha, 'A Note of Triumph: On *The Collected Poems*', in Paul Alexander (ed.), *Ariel Ascending: Writings about Sylvia Plath* (New York: Harper & Row, 1985), 94–9. A powerful defence for reading Plath's poetry separately from her biography.

Rose, Jacqueline, *The Haunting of Sylvia Plath* (London: Virago Press, 1991). An excellent psychoanalytic and deconstructive study on Sylvia Plath's writing and the archival work done on her biography.

Schwartz, Murray M., and Bollas, Christopher, 'The Absence at the Centre: Sylvia Plath and Suicide', in Gary Lane (ed.), *Sylvia Plath: New Views on the Poetry* (Baltimore: Johns Hopkins University Press, 1979), 179–202. A useful discussion of the way Plath's theme of suicidal urge and rebirth is cast within the context of her poetic reworking of the family.

Steiner, George, 'Dying is an Art', in Steiner, *Language and Silence* (Faber & Faber, 1967), 324–31. A sympathetic article addressing Plath's usage of holocaust imagery in her late poems.

Stevenson, Anne, *Bitter Fame: A Life of Sylvia Plath* (New York: Viking, 1989). One of several recent biographies, highlighting Plath's ruthlessly self-absorbed traits, her ambitions, her jealousies, and her psychic fragilities.

—— 'Sylvia Plath and the Romantic Heritage', *PN Review*, 16/6 (1990), 18–21. An article reading Plath's work in the context of romantic imagination.

Thompson, Catherine, ' "Dawn Poems in Blood": Sylvia Plath and PMS', *Triquarterly*, 80 (1990/1), 221–20. Thompson offers further material for the writing of Plath's biography, suggesting that Plath's psychic anguish should be seen in relation to hormonal disorders in connection with premenstrual syndrome.

Van Dyne, Susan, 'Fueling the Phoenix Fire: The Manuscripts of Sylvia Plath's "Lady Lazarus"', *Massachusetts Review*, 24 (1983), 395–410. A precise analysis of Plath's work sheets of 'Lady Lazarus' aimed at illustrating the inextricable conjunction between resurrection and self-destruction played through in this poem.

Wagner, Linda W., 'Plath's "Ladies Home Journal" Syndrome', *Journal of American Culture*, 7 (1984), 32–8. Wagner offers a discussion of Plath's work in the context of 1950s popular culture.

—— 'Sylvia Plath's Specialness in her Short Stories', *Journal of Narrative Technique*, 15 (Winter 1985), 1–14. A discussion of the theme of cultural alienation in Plath's prose writing.

Wagner-Martin, Linda, *Sylvia Plath: A Biography* (New York: Simon & Schuster, 1987). A biography concentrating on the conflicts facing Plath as a woman writer.

Yalom, Marilyn, 'Sylvia Plath, *The Bell Jar*, and Related Poems', in Diane Wood Middlebrook and Marilyn Yalom (eds.), *Coming to Light: American Women Poets in the Twentieth Century* (Ann Arbor, Mich.: University of Michigan Press, 1985), 167–94. A useful article on Plath's reworking of her relation to her parents in her writing.

Young, James E., *Writing and Rewriting the Holocaust: Narrative and the Consequences of Interpretation* (Bloomington, Ind.: Indiana University Press, 1988). An excellent defence of Plath's usage of holocaust imagery in her late poetry.

BACKGROUND READING

Abraham, Nicolas, and Torok, Maria, *The Shell and the Kernel*, i, ed., trans., and with an introduction by Nicholas T. Rand (Chicago: University of Chicago Press, 1994).

Barthes, Roland, 'Myth Today', in *A Barthes Reader*, ed. Susan Sontag, trans. Richard Howard (New York: Hill & Wang, 1982), 93–149.

—— *Roland Barthes*, trans. Richard Howard (New York: Hill & Wang, 1977).

Blanchot, Maurice, *The Gaze of Orpheus and Other Literary Essays*, trans. Lydia Davis (Barrytown: Station Hill Press, 1981).

Braudy, Leo, *The Frenzy of Renown: Fame and its History* (New York/ Oxford: Oxford University Press, 1986).

Bronfen, Elisabeth, *Over her Dead Body: Death Femininity and the Aesthetic* (Manchester: Manchester University Press, 1992).

—— *The Knotted Subject: Hysteria and its Discontents* (Princeton: Princeton University Press, 1998).

Butler, Judith, *Bodies that Matter: On the Discursive Limits of 'Sex'* (New York: Routledge, 1993).

Cavell, Stanley, *Disowning Knowledge in Six Plays of Shakespeare* (Cambridge: Cambridge University Press, 1987).

de Lauretis, Teresa, *Alice Doesn't: Feminism, Semiotics, Cinema* (Bloomington: Ind.: Indiana University Press, 1984).

de Man, Paul, *The Rhetoric of Romanticism* (New York: Colombia University Press, 1984).

Foucault, Michel, *Language, Counter-memory, Practice: Selected Essays and Interviews*, ed. and trans. Donald F. Bouchard with Sherry Simon (Ithaca, NY: Cornell University Press, 1977).

Freud, Sigmund, with Breuer, Josef, *Studies in Hysteria* (Standard Edition, 2; London: Hogarth Press, 1955).

—— 'Mourning and Melancholia' (Standard Edition, 14; London: Hogarth Press, 1957), 237–60.

—— *Beyond the Pleasure Principle* (Standard Edition, 18; London: Hogarth Press, 1955), 1–64.

—— 'Fetishism' (Standard Edition, 21; London: Hogarth Press, 1961), 149–57.

Homans, Margaret, *Women Writers and Poetic Identity* (Princeton: Princeton University Press, 1980).

Irigaray, Luce, *Speculum of the Other Woman*, trans. Gillian Gill (Ithaca, NY: Cornell University Press, 1985).

Israël, Lucien, *L'Hystérique, le sexe et le médicin* (Paris: Masson, 1976).

Johnson, Barbara, *A World of Difference* (Baltimore: Johns Hopkins University Press, 1987).

Kristeva, Julia, *Powers of Horror: An Essay on Abjection*, trans. Leon S. Roudiez (New York: Columbia University Press, 1982).

—— *Revolution in Poetic Language*, trans. Margaret Waller (New York: Columbia University Press, 1984).

—— *Black Sun: Depression and Melancholia*, trans. Leon S. Roudiez (New York: Columbia University Press, 1989).

Lacan, Jacques, 'Intervention on Transference', in Charles Bernheimer and Claire Kahane (eds.)., *In Dora's Case: Freud–Hysteria–Feminism* (Ithaca, NY: Cornell University Press, 1985), 94–104.

—— 'On a Question Preliminary to any Possible Treatment of Psychosis', in Lacan, *Écrits: A Selection*, ed. Alan Sheridan (New York: Norton, 1977), 179–225.

Levine, Michael G., *Writing through Repression: Literature, Censorship, Psychoanalysis* (Baltimore: Johns Hopkins University Press, 1994).

Moers, Ellen, *Literary Women: The Great Writers* (New York: Doubleday, 1977).

Montefiore, Jan, *Feminism and Poetry: Language, Experience, Identity in Women's Writing* (London: Pandora, 1994).

Santner, Eric L., *My Own Private Germany: Daniel Paul Schreber's Secret History of Modernity* (Princeton: Princeton University Press, 1996).

Showalter, Elaine, *The Female Malady: Women, Madness, and English Culture, 1830–1980* (New York, Pantheon Books, 1985).

Trillat, Étienne, *Histoire de l'hystérie* (Paris: Seghers, 1986).

Veith, Ilza, *Hysteria: The History of a Disease* (Chicago: University of Chicago Press, 1965).

Vernant, Jean-Pierre, 'Figuration de l'invisible et catégorie psychologique du double: Le Colossus', in Vernant, *Mythe & pensée chez les Grecs* (Paris: La Découverte, 1988), 325–38.

Wysocki, Gisela von, 'Das Leben: Ein hektisches Dabeigewesensein', *Die Zeit*, 15 (4 Apr. 1997), 53.

Zizek, Slavoj, *Enjoy your Symptom: Jacques Lacan in Hollywood and out* (New York: Routledge, 1992).

—— *The Indivisible Remainder: An Essay of Schelling and Related Matters* (London: Verso, 1996).

Index

*Recent and
Forthcoming Titles
in the
New Series of*

WRITERS AND
THEIR WORK

WRITERS AND THEIR WORK
RECENT & FORTHCOMING TITLES

RECENT & FORTHCOMING TITLES

Title	Author
Sylvia Plath	*Elisabeth Bronfen*
Jean Rhys	*Helen Carr*
Richard II	*Margaret Healy*
Dorothy Richardson	*Carol Watts*
John Wilmot, Earl of Rochester	*Germaine Greer*
Romeo and Juliet	*Sasha Roberts*
Christina Rossetti	*Kathryn Burlinson*
Salman Rushdie	*Damian Grant*
Paul Scott	*Jacqueline Banerjee*
The Sensation Novel	*Lyn Pykett*
P.B. Shelley	*Paul Hamilton*
Wole Soyinka	*Mpalive Msiska*
Edmund Spenser	*Colin Burrow*
J.R.R. Tolkien	*Charles Moseley*
Leo Tolstoy	*John Bayley*
Charles Tomlinson	*Tim Clark*
Anthony Trollope	*Andrew Sanders*
Victorian Quest Romance	*Robert Fraser*
Angus Wilson	*Peter Conradi*
Mary Wollstonecraft	*Jane Moore*
Virginia Woolf	*Laura Marcus*
Working Class Fiction	*Ian Haywood*
W.B. Yeats	*Edward Larrissy*
Charlotte Yonge	*Alethea Hayter*

TITLES IN PREPARATION

Title	Author
Chinua Achebe	*Yousef Nahem*
Antony and Cleopatra	*Ken Parker*
Jane Austen	*Meenakshi Mukherjee*
Pat Barker	*Sharon Monteith*
Samuel Beckett	*Keir Elam*
John Betjeman	*Dennis Brown*
William Blake	*John Beer*
Elizabeth Bowen	*Maud Ellmann*
Charlotte Brontë	*Sally Shuttleworth*
Lord Byron	*Drummond Bone*
Daniel Defoe	*Jim Rigney*
Charles Dickens	*Rod Mengham*
Early Modern Sonneteers	*Michael Spiller*
T.S. Eliot	*Colin MacCabe*
Brian Friel	*Geraldine Higgins*
The *Gawain* Poetry	*John Burrow*
The Georgian Poets	*Rennie Parker*
Henry IV	*Peter Bogdanov*
Henry V	*Robert Shaughnessy*
Geoffrey Hill	*Andrew Roberts*
Christopher Isherwood	*Stephen Wade*
Kazuo Ishiguro	*Cynthia Wong*
Ben Jonson	*Anthony Johnson*
John Keats	*Kelvin Everest*
Charles and Mary Lamb	*Michael Baron*
Langland: *Piers Plowman*	*Claire Marshall*
Language Poetry	*Alison Mark*
Macbeth	*Kate McCluskie*
Katherine Mansfield	*Helen Haywood*
Harold Pinter	*Mark Batty*
Alexander Pope	*Pat Rogers*
Dennis Potter	*Derek Paget*
Religious Poets of the 17th Century	*Helen Wilcox*
Revenge Tragedy	*Janet Clare*
Richard III	*Edward Burns*
Siegfried Sassoon	*Jenny Hartley*
Mary Shelley	*Catherine Sharrock*
Stevie Smith	*Alison Light*
Muriel Spark	*Brian Cheyette*
Gertrude Stein	*Nicola Shaughnessy*
Laurence Sterne	*Manfred Pfister*
Tom Stoppard	*Nicholas Cadden*
The Tempest	*Gordon McMullan*
Tennyson	*Seamus Perry*
Derek Walcott	*Stewart Brown*
John Webster	*Thomas Sorge*
Edith Wharton	*Janet Beer*
Women Playwrights of the 1980s	*Dimple Godiwala*
Women Romantic Poets	*Anne Janowitz*
Women Writers of Gothic Literature	*Emma Clery*
Women Writers of the 17th Century	*Ramona Wray*
Women Writers of the Late 19th Century	*Gail Cunningham*